Sunburnt Pom's
Tales of Oz

Sunburnt Pom's
Tales of Oz

Mark Harland

Published by MVH Publishing

A CIP catalogue record for this book is available from the British Library.

ISBN 978-0-9935895-6-0 (ePub)
ISBN 978-0-9935895-7-7 (mobi)
ISBN 978-0-9935895-8-4 (paperback)

Book layout and design by Clare Brayshaw

Prepared and printed by:

York Publishing Services Ltd
64 Hallfield Road
Layerthorpe
York
YO31 7ZQ

Tel: 01904 431213

Website: www.yps-publishing.co.uk

CONTENTS

AUTHOR'S NOTE

Our family connections with Australia go back a long way. There were rumours of 'interesting characters' on Dad's side of the family who sought new lives under the guidance of His Majesty in both North America and further east, so to speak. The family name of Cody features prominently on my paternal grandmother's family tree: so you get the general drift. However, it wasn't until 1943 when my father Vic, his brother Bernard and brother-in-law Reg arrived Down Under with the British Pacific Fleet, that normal relations were established with the Lucky Country.

So after listening to numerous tales and anecdotes from three English sailors about the Island continent and its people there had to come a time to find out for myself. These little stories are all true and I hope you enjoy reading them as much as I did writing them. I have tried to come up with a single word that epitomises the Australian character. How can any writer use one word to sum up 'friendly, humorous, dry, quick witted and laconic?' It certainly has me beaten. To fully understand what I mean, you'll have to go Down Under yourself – that is if you haven't been already.

My thanks go to Barry Nankervis of Bendigo, once again, for advice on all matters Australian, and to Annie Roberts of Mollymook NSW whose own enthusiasm for this book ensured it was completed with a minimum of errors. I owe you both a few cold ones!

I have made two longish trips to Oz. Will I go again? You just try stopping me. Who knows, there might even be further tales to write. I sure hope so.

Mark Harland
AKA the 'Sunburnt Pom.'

WHAT KIND OF BISCUITS?

It was by far the longest sector I had ever flown. Dubai to Perth. I was about to fulfil a lifelong ambition and fly to Australia. A combination of various circumstances had made it impossible until now but finally here I was in the Economy section of an Emirates 777 heading south-east over the Indian Ocean. The two passengers to my left were a young girl called Jenny and her father Mike who had emigrated from Lincolnshire to Perth. They had been back visiting his parents in the 'Old Country' during the long Aussie summer holiday and were looking forward to going home to Kwinana. Jenny was a little chatterbox telling me all sorts of stories about where they lived but finally the combination of body clock and darkness took its toll and she fell asleep. It was time for some other form of flight entertainment. I switched on the console in front of me and within seconds realised I needed the assistance of a ten-year-old girl who had just fallen asleep. Having mastered the console on the 'outward' leg, Jenny was now a veteran. A sleeping veteran.

I played with a few knobs and switches and found myself in the 'flight information' section. Emirates have on-board cameras that allow you to see below and ahead of the aircraft which gives you a bird-in-the-sky feeling. It was terrific and a few hours earlier I had watched the coastline of the Oman disappear beneath us as the view became ocean. Then it dawned on me that there would be nothing to see until we met landfall in Western Australia in about another ten hours time. Ten hours! I think it was only then that the remoteness of the Island Continent that is Australia struck home. I found a 'moving map' display; which showed a map of the Middle East and the Arabian Peninsula. A little white arrow with wings depicted our plane with its nose pointing south-east. In its path was....absolutely nothing. Where was Australia? I switched to 'Sector Information' which was equally depressing. Distance to destination … ten zillion kilometres. Time to destination … more than enough to ask for Dr Who's intervention. Oh well, maybe a read or something? I am normally a fan of in-flight airline magazines but the problem with the bigger international airlines is that their magazines tend to emulate *National Geographic* with pictures of their newest jets landing here there and everybloodywhere. Interspersed of course with advertisements to sell you everything you don't need at six miles above the ocean like expensive chronometers guaranteed to be waterproof six miles below it. My favourite airlines are those that sell you nothing except good service and the products and attractions of their own nation. So that rules most of them out!

Fortunately I had brought with me in my flight bag a pre-production proof copy of my first novel – *Your Country Needs You*. It had arrived from York Publishing Services on the morning of my departure along with a cheeky note from a Director, Duncan Beal.

'You can read this trash on the plane, it'll kill time. Have fun. Dunc.'

Indeed it would. It was the last opportunity to correct any errors which always seem to creep in no matter how many times a book is proof-read. I ordered a large gin and tonic from a stewardess who, despite her Scouse accent, did a passable imitation of a subservient Bedouin girl taking refreshments to her Emir. You have to laugh. I got stuck into the opening chapters with a red pen in one hand and the gin in the other. Two hours, a few red circles and several gins later later I was approaching about half-way in the book. I needed a pee, a glass of water and a break. I put the book into the pouch in front along with the safety instructions, flight mag and puke bag and made my way to the facilities. Chilled water was available via a bulkhead mounted container and those awful tiny conical cardboard cups that barely hold a mouthful before you have to refill them. I did so three times. Then it ran out. I pointed this out to another Bedouin wannabee of indeterminate nationality who shrugged her shoulders and just smiled. I ordered a beer and returned to my seat. It would be only another day or two before I came to learn that most beer in Australia is served in glasses only marginally bigger than those plastic cones used for dispensing water. 'Drink plenty of water to avoid dehydrating during the flight' it had said in the magazine. And here they were either rationing or running out of the stuff! Oh well.

Before recommencing the reading I decided to take another look at the map display. Big mistake. I was hoping to see the whole of Australia on the map with our little white plane happily pinging its merry way Down Under but the only visible part of Oz was a bulge on the west side and it was right inside the bottom right-hand corner of the map. Unless you knew it could only be Australia you wouldn't think it was. Distance to destination … seven zillion kilometres. Time to destination … seven hours etc. Matilda and Men at Work seemed as far away as ever. I carried on reading, not having to trouble the red pen too often, thankfully. Eventually I finished and put the book and myself to bed. Apart from the pilots, I hope, I think I was only person still awake.

I was awoken by the sound of the clanking of food trays. Breakfast was being served. Or was it lunch, supper or whatever? All sense of time and distance had evaporated. Whatever it was Jenny was wide awake and looking at her map display and eager to educate me. By now Australia had morphed into most of a continent with only only the east coast yet to appear. Progress!

'We live just......here!' shrieked Jenny as she stuck her thumb onto a chunk of coastline but such was the diminished scale that even her little thumb probably covered a half a million square miles, iron ore mountains and several gold fields. I was only just beginning to get the feeblest of grips on the sheer size of Western Australia which is itself about a third of the total land mass and the biggest State by far of the six that together form the Commonwealth of Australia.

With the meal over, I too consulted the Flight Information on the console and was delighted to learn there was less than a thousand kilometres to reach Perth, terra firma. In fact, very shortly afterwards the Captain's voice came over the tannoy and I was slightly amused to hear a Dutch or Belgian twang to the well-spoken voice. I say amused because as a regular passenger on the Hull to Zeebrugge ferry crossing most of the Captains' announcements have that Flemish lilt where most nouns are spoken as if they are all plural. When a Captain announces his name as a Van den Something you always know you are in for a linguistic treat. This was no exception.

'Good eveningsh. Captain Victor Vandenbroucke shpeaking to you from the flight decksh. We shall be

4

landingsh in Perths in about one hour's time. All non-Australiansh will be required to complete a questionnaire to preshent to Immigrations Offishers. I hope you have enjoyed the flightsh. Cabin shtaff will be making a money collection for the airline's sponsored charity which this year is Water Aid and...'

He had to be joking. Water Aid?! Well they sure needed aid with water on board this kite. No wonder I'd had to drink so much gin and beer. Maybe it was someone's idea of a laugh. If it was, I take my hat off to them. We followed the WA coast line south and very soon I could see the lights of Perth in the distance through the window to port. I immediately recalled the words of the American astronaut, John Glenn, who when he had orbited the Earth five decades earlier had described Perth as the 'City of Lights'. John died only a few weeks before I wrote this story. What a great guy he was. Regarding his epic journey as a start in life and not a pinnacle, he went on to become a well-respected Congressman representing the State of Ohio. Whether he ever visited Perth, on the ground so to speak, I don't know. I sure hope so because he was the first internationally recognised person to put Perth on the map.

We landed, descending from the ocean heading north-east and taxied to the terminal. For some reason I was one of the last to clear Immigration. The officer, John from his name badge, was in his sixties and very friendly.

'Good morning, how are you, Mr Harland.' He already had my passport opened.

'Tired but happy, thank you. Glad to be here.' I was, too.

'What do you write?' This confused me and my quizzical gaze brought forth a response.

'You're a writer. At least that's what you put on the Immigration Form under occupation.'

Had I? I must have done it under the influence of gin and jet lag. Mind you, it was partially true. I had, after all, just written my first novel.

'Oh yeah. This is my first book here.' I reached into my bag and pulled it out, showing it to him. To my astonishment he reached across the counter, took it in his hand and started to read the back cover, which was a synopsis of the story.

'Wow, so you've written a book about dodgy politicians, have you?'

He started to take a note of the title, publisher etc. writing it down on a pad. Don't tell me I was already under suspicion for something! Why else would he be doing this? I needn't have worried and my concern was short-lived.

'When does it come out this book here in Australia? We've got got more 'dodgy pollies' here in Australia than anywhere else, believe me. You should write your next book here, mate.'

He smiled, handed me the book and my passport back and to my amazement stuck his hand out to shake mine.

'Welcome to Australia, enjoy your first visit and make sure you come again, mate.'

I was almost bowled over. Customs Control was an entirely different experience. Having collected my trusty Delsey suitcase from the luggage carousel we were split into two lines – those with 'Food to Declare' and those that didn't. My friend Lynne had warned me about this when she had asked me to bring her mum some English biscuits. I heard a very loud and officious female voice barking at a couple of passengers in front of me. The Customs Officer was around fifty, obviously liked her food and had a gun holstered onto a wide leather belt. A gun for God's sake. What were they expecting, a mass delivery of coke? And I don't mean Diet Coke.

'Next. What have you got to declare?'

'Good morning. I've got two packets of biscuits for a little old lady in Balca...'

'Right, mate. Exactly what kind of biscuits?'

This was not what I was expecting. 'Er, they're Marks & Spencer's custard creams.'

'That's OK. No worries. Straight on. Next!'

I often wonder what would have happened if I had said 'Jammy Dodgers' or 'Ginger Nuts'.

It does make you wonder. Welcome to Australia indeed. It was going to be an interesting three weeks and in the event I would enjoy every second of it. Well almost every second of it, as the following nineteen stories will demonstrate. Happy reading!

BOUTIQUE BEER?

I had been in Australia twenty-four hours, well almost, and I still hadn't had a beer. This was a disaster. As a Pom influenced by a naval father, grandfather and three naval uncles to believe that Oz was the land of heavy drinking Okkers, I couldn't wait to meet and drink with these stereotyped characters for real. The *Adventures of Barry McKenzie* and countless TV ads for the Amber Nectar, Castlemaine XXXX, Resch's (more bounce to the ounce!) and VB had simply whetted my 'ebb tide' for the day I would have my first beer Down Under. And here I was in Western Australia, home of the famous Swan Lager, which as a mark of respect to the locals I would drink first and raise a glass to all my forbears who had passed through this part of the Lucky Country.

'We're going to a jazz session tonight in Northbridge, Mark. The session starts at seven so we'll leave here at six-thirty, OK?'

Now my host Lynne, lovely girl though she is, was a 'cuppa tea' kind of girl, not beer. Her fridge was full of cat food, milk and the odd banana. A few tinnies of Swan Lager would have looked as out of place and unwelcome as a pork chop on the Wailing Wall. But when in Rome, etc., so tea it was for the first twelve hours. I had an idea.

'How about I walk to the nearest pub en route, have a few cold ones, and you pick me up from there in your car?'

'No worries. I expect you're looking forward to your first beer here.'

That was the gross understatement of the year, although to be fair we hadn't seen January out yet.

'The Roundhouse is the nearest pub about 1km up the Wanneroo Road on the right by the Northlands shopping centre. You can't miss it.'

At about five-thirty I came in from the garden and the twelfth 'cuppa' that day to get showered and changed and ready to go out.

'You can't wear shorts to the Jazz Club! It's long strides only and a proper shirt.'

She had to be joking, surely. Was I really in Australia? The land of Ned Kelly, Banjo Patterson, cold beer and hot Sheilas? I was beginning to wonder if Waltzing Matilda might have to be rewritten in a more PC version. I just did as I was told and went to put on some Chinos, sports shirt (with collar) and brown hush puppies.

'That's better, Mark. I'll pick you up from the pub in about forty-five minutes.'

And with that she disappeared to perform her own makeover from girl next door to girl about town. I turned up the road and then left onto the Wanneroo Road and crossed over to be on the correct side when I got there. It was still bloody hot and the sun had barely started to dip and turn to the left. It was my first experience of the sun being in the wrong place at the wrong time with me being a southern hemisphere virgin so to speak. I regretted not bringing my sunnies (sun glasses to any Pom readers), and the hot air still shimmered off the road like it does in the movies where folk get lost in the bush and die. I squinted my way north for the required distance and immediately found the Roundhouse which was correctly named by its shape. I couldn't find the way in at first as amazingly the building was split into four separate businesses, each having, presumably, ninety degrees of the circle. The first door I went through was the wrong one and I immediately found myself in a betting shop. A few wall-mounted screens showed some live racing from somewhere with just a handful of men watching. I made enquiries.

'The pub's next door mate. No worries.'

In fact it was next-door-but-one and occupied between 180 degrees and 270 degrees if you get my geometrical analogy. Maybe the pub should have been called the Euclid Arms or something. I went in and was gobsmacked to see only one other customer, a male aged about seventy sat at the bar immediately opposite a TV screen depicting, I think, the same race I had seen moments earlier in the zero to 90 degrees betting shop. He had an almost-full if small glass of beer in one hand and just gazed at the screen with a thousand mile stare. He didn't move a muscle. I walked to the bar where a young chap aged about eighteen and a day was serving. He certainly wouldn't be overworked that evening. He seemed friendly enough.

'Hi, what can I get you?'

This was a huge moment for me and one I wanted to savour. 'Hi, for my first ever beer in Australia I would like a pint of your finest Swan Lager please. As cold as you can get it.'

'Sorry, a what did you say mate?'

'A Swan Lager, you know, your local brew.' He looked puzzled.

'Sorry. I don't think we sell that any more. Not for a long time now. No demand for it mate. We only sell boutique beers here now.'

I could not believe my ears. I was stunned and wasn't sure how to respond. 'What the heck is a boutique beer?'

There was no time for the young chap to even reply. Suddenly the previously-silent bloke at the bar, obviously the worse for liquid wear, shouted out:

'I'm telling yer mate. The whole bloody country's gone to the bloody dogs. Australia's run by a bunch of poofters now mate!'

And that was all he ever said. His eyes never left the screen depicting the racing from the local Gloucester Park. I had no option but to drink a boutique beer at an extortionate price from a ridiculously small glass. Sad to say but I can't even remember its name. I think I downed three or four before Lynne arrived to take me into Northbridge. The Jazz Club was great, the company uplifting, and the cold Swan Lager even better. My faith in Australia had been restored. Boutique beers my arse!

YOU NEW ROUND HERE?

'The best way into the city, Mark, is to get the bus to Stirling station and take the TransPerth train into the CBD. The bus stop is round the corner on the Wanneroo Road. They run all day. Gotta go to work. Must dash. See you later.'

I was staying with my friend Lynne in Balcatta, a northern suburb of Perth. Having arrived from England only forty-eight hours earlier, I was still jet-lagged and unaccustomed to the heat which in late January was fierce. The contrast with the freezing, foggy Yorkshire I had left behind could not have been greater. I got plastered up with sun cream and with 'sunnies' in place and a bottle of cold water in my small knapsack I stepped out the front door. Whammo! The heat hit me straight away and it was still only just after eight o'clock. I pulled my cheap sun hat even further down over my eyes and nose until I could only just see where I was going. Lynne had given me rough directions to find the bus stop.

'Turn right at the roundabout up Beryl Street and walk up to the main Wanneroo Road, turn left and keep walking till you see the bus stop', she had said the previous evening – in marked contrast to the 'round the corner' this morning.

Distances don't mean a lot to Aussies, I was soon to discover. 'Up the road' could mean a block or two away or it could be Geraldton three hundred kilometres up the coast. I soon found Beryl Street and the Wanneroo Road, turned left and kept walking. It was reassuring that I could see the glass bus shelter glinting in the sun about two hundred metres away. However when I got there I was shocked to discover that it had obviously been vandalised very recently as there was broken glass all over the pavement and in the gutter. I thought I had left all that sort of nonsense behind me in the UK. I searched in vain for some sort of timetable that you would normally expect to see in an English bus shelter. Zilch! I looked at my watch. It was eight-fifteen.

Behind the shelter on the other side of a newly-constructed brick wall about a metre high was a building site where it looked like about a dozen new 'Yew Nuts' were being constructed. A 'Yew Nut' is a small townhouse, or unit, built by the thousand in the suburbs of all Australia's major cities and conurbations. In England we would probably call them 'starter homes', although I soon discovered that in Australia many retired and elderly folk also lived in them so they could equally be called 'finishing homes' I thought.

I sat on the wall and waited. Twenty minutes later there was still no sign of a bus. In fact there was hardly any traffic at all, just the odd 'Ute passing by. I was startled by a loud male voice behind me.

'Are you waiting for a bus, mate? You might have a long wait. They're only every hour from what I can tell, mate.'

'Oh heck, is that right? Thanks for the info.' He seemed eager to help and was obviously a bricklayer, judging from the steel trowel in his right hand.

'Yih, where do you want to go, mate?'

'Stirling train station, then into the City.'

'Are you new round here, mate?'

'You could say that. I flew in from Yorkshire a couple of days ago.'

'First trip to Australia?'

'Yes. It sure is hot. Look what happened to the bus shelter. It's all smashed up. Vandals?'

'No mate, looks like it was hit by a hoon last night.' The word was lost on me and I cast him a quizzical look.

'You know mate – a young tearaway driver probably on drugs or drink and showing off in front of his mates. Anyway, mate, you need to get to Stirling. If the bus doesn't come soon I'll gladly give you a lift in my 'Ute during my smoko.'

Having learnt much basic Strine before leaving the UK thanks to a book called *Let Stalk Strine* by Afferbeck Lauder, I knew that a 'smoko' was a fag and tea break. How kind was that? I had been Down Under for five minutes and already a bloke on a building site was offering a total stranger a lift. He kept chatting as the brick wall grew brick by brick. He told me that the previous year he had visited rellies in Yorkshire and had even taken in a four-day cricket match. He said he was frozen all the time he was there despite it being in July. Suddenly I heard the noise of a bus coming and I picked up my bag.

Thanks for your offer, my friend. Cheerio.'

'Just tell the driver you're new round here and he'll put you right, mate.' He waved with his trowel.

The bus slowed to a halt and I climbed aboard to find there were only three or four other passengers. To my surprise the driver turned the engine off.

'Yih, where to, mate?'

'Stirling train station please.'

'Jew wanna come back?'

'Well yes, I'd like to if that's all right?'

'Where do you really wanna go, mate? Are you new round here?'

'Yes, I'm visiting from England. I want to go into the City then come back here late afternoon.'

'Well why didn't you bloody say? Anyway no worries. It's all TransPerth now mate so I can give you one ticket for two bus rides and two train rides. Seven dollars please mate.'

I paid up and took a seat. The other passengers looked at me, smiled and then carried on talking. They obviously knew each other. The driver restarted the engine and we headed north up the Wanneroo Road. To my amazement we stopped again about three hundred yards up the road outside a smart bungalow where an elderly lady was watering roses in the front garden. The driver got out and went to talk to her.

'G'day Joyce. Just thought I'd stop to ask how Charlie is after his operation?'

I'd heard that everyone in Western Australia was laid back, but this was beyond belief. I very quickly learnt that the letters WA really stand for 'Wait Awhile'.

A full five minutes later, and satisfied that Charlie was in recovery mode, the driver got back on board. Just before he started the engine a loud but squeaky voice came over a speaker. It was the controller from the bus depot.

'Attention bus number five. Your bus is stationary. Do you have a problem?'

'No worries, mate. I just stopped to see how Charlie was getting on – you know after his operation and all.'

'Yih right, mate. How is he?'

'Joyce says he doing well.'

'Pass on all our best wishes but step on it mate you're running twenty minutes late already.'

'No, I'm forty minutes early for the next one.'

We all heard the mike click off at the depot.

'Bastards. Since all these satellite tracker things were fitted they know exactly where you are. Anyway at least they asked about Charlie. Hopefully he'll be back to work soon.'

I could only assume that Charlie was a fellow bus driver. Twenty minutes later we finally arrived at Stirling train station, which wasn't all that far away from Stirling City Hall, a local administrative building, Stirling being one of twelve Cities that make up Greater Perth. The station was simply amazing and was constructed above the parallel tracks that took trains north and south down the centre of a six-lane motorway, three heading north and three heading south to the City. How simple was that, and how innovative?

I walked up a flight of concrete steps and followed the sign that said 'Trains to Perth' and taking care not to follow the 'Trains to Joondalup and Clarkson' which were presumably heading north. I immediately started singing the Monkees tune '*Take the last train to Clarksville*', mentally substituting Clarkson. Just to make sure I asked a uniformed attendant to put me right.

'Are you new round here mate?'

BLUEYS

'I thought we'd go to the beach today, Mark' announced my host one morning after breakfast and all four cats had been fed. Combined, they ate a lot more than she did, that's for sure.

As I was still 'new round here', the beaches of WA within four days drive of Perth would not have been my chosen subject on Mastermind, if you get my drift. 'Scuse the pun.

'So, Mark, we can go to Scarborough Beach, Trigg, Cottesloe or Sorrento. You're the visitor so you choose.'

Having been to Sorrento, Italy several times as a youngster owing to our family living in nearby Malta, I opted for its namesake. It would be good to compare the two. It was still early by my standards anyway, probably about nineish. Armed with lots of cold water, sun cream, beach towels, beach mats and sunnies (sun glasses), we set off in Lynne's beat-up old Suzuki jeep which, to be fair, should have been consigned to a museum many years earlier. There wasn't a lot of wear left on the clutch to put it mildly, and every gear change was an assault on the ear drums.

It took about half an hour to get there and I was impressed with many of the properties actually built on the coast road facing the Indian Ocean and for the most part looking big and expensive. Many flew Australian flags from their rooftops and balconies in a show of patriotic fervour during and following the very recent Australia Day national holiday. What a happy contrast to England where until so recently EU flags took precedence over that of St. George.

We parked in a huge car park that obviously was shared with the proximate Hillary's Boat Harbour. It was packed despite the still early hour.

'Yih, lots of folk like to come down to the beach before it gets too hot, Mark. Make sure you've got plenty of sun block on.'

It was probably already about 35C. We 'made camp' on the beach about thirty metres from the water's edge. There was a slight swell with waves probably about the one metre mark breaking onto the golden sands at regular intervals about every fifteen seconds. Not enough to entice any 'surfies', that's for sure, and there were certainly none in the water that I could see. Lynne did not like direct sun and sat on a beach mat wearing sunnies and a white towel wrapped over her head and shoulders, looking like a superannuated Emirates air hostess. It didn't look as if the ocean was going to attract her, at least not for the immediate future. Not having swum in the Indian Ocean since an enforced and prolonged refuelling stop on the Island of Gan over three decades earlier, I was keen to renew my acquaintance with the world's second biggest stretch of salt water.

There were a few people in the water but not many. I stripped off to my white trunks and decided there was only one way to do this and that was to run in straight and shallow-dive into a breaking wave. So I did. It was freezing! I just couldn't believe how cold the water felt. It was probably the contrast with the open air temperature of 40C and the water temperature of 20C that caused goose bumps to erupt over my entire torso. Unfazed and showing a brave face, I struck out west towards South Africa, well maybe fifty metres of the journey anyway. I had probably only been in the water about five minutes when suddenly a swimmer travelling at great speed towards the beach passed extremely close to me. He had a bathing cap on, a swimming vest that looked like medieval chain mail and goggles, and was doing about three knots like an Olympian. If only I could swim like that. As he drew level with me and his mouth broke the surface for the latest gulp of fuelling oxygen he suddenly shouted out:

'Look out mate, I just spotted a couple of blueys!'

I froze solid, the goose pimples re-erupting like miniature volcanos, confirming that we were in Sorrento after all and within sight of Vesuvius herself. Blue sharks! Not exactly great whites or tiger sharks but big enough to take a leg off in one bite. Instantly, memories of watching *Blue Water, White Death* and Steven Spielberg's *Jaws* flashed through my mind. I could almost hear the terrifying sound track so characteristic of the latter – dum dum, dum dum, dum dum....- as my sphincter muscles went into overdrive. Fortunately so did my arms, which immediately resembled the paddle wheels of Mississippi riverboats. Mark Spitz, eat your heart out.

It probably took only two or three minutes to reach the safety of the beach but it seemed an eternity. I was mentally composing the headlines in the *Western Australian* the next day.

'Pommy tourist hit by shark at Sorrento' or 'Unlucky Pom is holiday season's first shark victim.'

It didn't happen. Arms and torso eventually met with coarse golden sand in about half a metre of water, and I staggered onto dry land, still shaking. The bloke who had given me the warning also appeared, removed his goggles and walked towards me.

'You did the right thing, mate. They can give you a very nasty sting indeed. You look as if you're new round here.'

'A sting, how do you mean?'

'Blueys. Bluebottles. All you can see on the surface is a small blue ball like a ping pong ball but underneath is about a metre of tail. Nastiest jellyfish in these parts I can tell you, mate. See ya.'

Jellyfish! Not blue sharks! Blue jellyfish. I didn't know whether to laugh or cry. In the event I went for a cold beer. I bloody needed it.

THE WALK

'I'll drop you up near Point Vernon straight after breakfast, Mark. You said you wanted a good walk. Just keep going until you get to Urangan Boat Harbour and me 'n' Paul will meet you there for lunch about oneish, OK?'

That was last night after a few scoops of Queen Charlotte chardonnay and probably a beer or two on top. What seemed like a good idea then did not seem quite such a good idea now. Although only about eight 'o' clock, it was stinking hot. I had about a litre of water, some sun cream and a tourist map of the 'Hervey Bay Area' in my knapsack. Pam's Kia disappeared into the heat haze and I was now on my own. There were a few houses built close to the water's edge. All I had to do was keep the ocean on my left and keep walking. It was scenic enough all right, and with the sun still rising on my left I knew I was heading more or less due south. The ocean, or rather the Coral Sea, was almost dead calm, and one of the advantages of having the Big Island (Fraser Island) ten miles to the east of you was that it physically blocked the big Pacific rollers that could do so much damage to the shoreline, especially if a cyclone was around.

So here I was, ten thousand miles away from home, taking a walk alongside the Coral Sea without a care in the world. The buildings soon petered out and it was just scrub and vegetation to my right and ocean to my left. For the most part there was sort of path on the ocean side of the road, not that there was much traffic to avoid anyway, just the odd car and a motor-home or two. Tourists from NSW probably making their way south after the Australia Day holidays. I kept walking. It got hotter and I kept swigging the water. It was probably only about nine 'o' clock and well over 30C I reckoned. Quite humid too, as Queensland can be. I had left the dry heat of WA back in Perth. I decided to take more care of the remaining water. There would surely be a café or something on the road soon. Surely!

My normal walking speed is about three knots, being a sailor's son, but the heat and humidity were now taking their toll. I stopped for more than the odd breather, and twice on a bridge that took the road over a small creek that would no doubt take rainwater into the sea. Always on the lookout for any of Australia's critters that could could hospitalise you or worse with just one bite, I peered into the shallow muddy waters but never spotted anything other than the occasional bird. Continuing on my by now not-so-merry way, and with the time probably about tennish, I spotted in the distance a Toyota Land Cruiser parked on a patch of flat ground on the landward side of the road. As I got closer I could see a bloke gazing up at a load of trees and taking notes on a clipboard. Life! I decided to ask this bloke how much further I had to go. He was presumably native to the area, a sort of Park Ranger type maybe?

'Excuse me. I am on the right road for Urangan Boat Harbour?' I pointed straight ahead.

'Yih, no worries on that one mate. Are you a visitor?'

'Yes, I'm staying with cousins in Pialba and we're meeting at the Boat Club for lunch. How long will it take me, roughly?'

'Fifteen to twenty minutes, mate, no worries. There's only one road, mate, just follow it. There's a café about 2k down the road owned by a Belgian bloke. You could maybe stop for a tea and a smoke. Nice place.'

'Thanks. I might just do that. Cheers.'

The stop would do me nicely and a cold beer or two and the chance to fill up my water bottle cheered me up immensely. With a spring in my step and with a cheery wave to the tree practitioner I headed off again. With the sun at almost full height on my left I knew I was heading due east. About ten minutes later the same Toyota came past me, then slowed down and stopped. As I drew level with it the nearside window was lowered and the 'Ranger' shouted out.

'Crikey mate, I thought you had a car. I meant twenty minutes in a car! I didn't know you were on foot!'

I didn't know what to say. Did he think I'd hidden 'my car' in the trees or somewhere when I spoke to him?

'Look mate, I can take you as far as Torquay, no worries. Then it's not too far from there. Yih?'

I was just beginning to wonder what the heck the English Riviera had to do with the edge of the Coral Sea when I noticed a single-storey building maybe two hundred metres in the distance. Unbelievably I could just make out the red, gold and black of a Belgian flag fluttering from a pole on the roof. As a frequent visitor to Bruges in Flanders, the flag was very familiar to me. I declined the offer of a lift. A glass or two of Jupiler pilsner or a Trappist ale sounded more attractive than a ride in a hot Land Cruiser.

Thanks for the offer but that must be the café you mentioned before. I'll refuel there and carry on.'

'No worries, your choice mate. G'day.'

The wry grin on his face troubled me slightly. I re-consulted the map that Pam had lent me. I soon found

Scarness and then Torquay on the map. Maybe the early explorers following Captain Cook had all started from Plymouth Hoe. I half expected to find Westward Ho! soon. They didn't look too far away and I reckoned that the Ranger had his times and distances confused. Even allowing for a 'tea break' I would be at the Boat Club well before the anticipated lunchtime. Or so I thought.

'So do you sell any Belgian beers here then?' The look on the assistant's face did not augur well I thought. Was he the proprietor? Had he even been to Belgium? I didn't even bother asking. If he was of Flemish descent then his name was probably Graeme or Bruce Vandenbroucke and he would be third-generation Oz. I had no wish to embarrass him.

'Two cold tinnies please mate, one glass and a litre bottle of mineral water please.'

'No worries.' This guy had never been anywhere near the Low Countries and in all probability had never left Queensland.

I sat outside and made polite conversation with a girl in her mid-twenties and her mother. They were from 'Sinny' and were driving back from a trip to the Whitsundays, a bunch of islands on the Great Barrier Reef 'just up the road', which is Ozspeak for about a thousand miles. It was probably about eleven o' clock when I set off again fuelled with two excellent cold VBs and with a fresh supply of cool water which I decanted into the lighter plastic bottle I had started the day with.

I kept walking and sure enough it started to get more like civilisation. There were more houses on the land side of the road, mostly built in the traditional Queenslander 'stilt style' with cars parked underneath. When I even reached some shops including of all things a butcher's, I reckoned that this must be Torquay. I was right too. From the map I would soon be at the Great White Shark Show (whatever that might be – the mind boggled) and from there a short hop to the Boat Harbour at Urangan. I reckoned that looking at the map I could save a mile or so by chopping off the headland and 'chucking a right' inland as they might say here in Oz.

The kilometre-long Urangan Pier looked interesting and I resolved to come back another day to walk its full length. A private house with the curious name of 'Asbestos Manor' tickled my sense of humour and I took a photo of the bright yellow Queenslander, whose owners obviously had a sense of humour as bright as the hue of their home. Soon enough I did 'chuck a right' and found myself in a road called Bruce Street. Was a Mr Bruce the original developer or had the town's naming committee been watching too much Monty Python? You just never knew in Australia.

I got lost, hopelessly lost. Like in the US very few people actually walk anywhere and although I did see a few people to ask, nobody knew where Urangan Boat Harbour was. I was gobsmacked, as we say in Yorkshire. I was within a mile, at the most, of Urangan Boat Harbour and nobody knew where it was. It wasn't as though there were lots of boat harbours. There was only one! I finally reached my destination. Unbelievably it was late afternoon. So much for lunch. Sheepishly I phoned Pam from the Club reception desk and she picked me up some twenty minutes later.

After supper and chilling with another litre of Queen Charlotte chardonnay, the topic of conversation inevitably got around to my walk. Did I enjoy it? Was it too hot? How many ks or miles had I walked? I retrieved the map from my knapsack, unfolded it and looked for the customary scale. There wasn't one. Cousin Paul had the last word.

'Mark, you do realise that that map Pam lent you is just a tourist attraction map, don't you? It's not to scale.'

Suddenly that wry grin on the Ranger's face made sense. He bloody knew!

JURASSIC PARK, OZ-STYLE

The chance to visit Fraser Island whilst staying with cousins Paul and Pam in Hervey Bay was just too good to miss. The 'Big Island', as the locals called it, was only thirty minutes away by 'barge' (strangest barge I've ever seen) so I pre-booked a day's excursion a few days before the trip itself.

At the unholy hour of about six in the morning Pam dropped me off at the pick-up point, a local hotel on the tourist circuit. I was the first aboard, and the driver introduced himself with a smile and a handshake.

'G'day, I'm Captain Kangaroo. Where are you from, mate?' This guy had to be joking, surely?

'Mark Harland. I'm from Scarborough, Yorkshire. What's your real name?'

'Everyone calls me Captain Kangaroo, mate. England eh? No worries. Take your pick of the seats, mate. Anywhere you like, mate.'

I sat near the back, probably out of habit from school days. We stopped at about six further pick-up points. With every new person the introduction was just the same.

'G'day, I'm Captain Kangaroo. Where are you from, mate?'

OK so he wasn't joking. I decided I liked this guy. There was no side to him at all. I smiled when the last two, a Japanese couple in their twenties, boarded the bus. They came and sat in the seats in front of me and smiled as they did so.

'Konichi wah.' I smiled back, having expended ten percent of my Japanese vocabulary with this simple greeting of Good Morning.

Miss Nip was over the moon and extended her hand Western style. Mr Nip was not amused and fiddled with one of several huge cameras slung around his neck. Suddenly Captain Kangaroo came over the tannoy.

'That's it, we're all aboard now. We head straight for the 'Landing' now and we'll be there in about twenty minutes.'

We drove south with the ocean on our left and Fraser Island visible as a huge green lump maybe eight or ten miles away. It was quite scenic, and we passed through a few small townships with pretty bungalows and manicured lawns. It seemed quite English apart from the heat. The departure point was no more than a concrete slipway with a few run-down single storey buildings nearby. Our vessel ("the barge") was parked nose hard on to the slipway with its landing-craft type bow door lowered onto the concrete. There were already several vehicles aboard her, including a small khaki coloured bus that looked as if it was Australian Army WW2 surplus. Maybe it was, you just never know in Australia, particularly Queensland, which ranks as the second quirkiest State, after Tasmania of course.

Our own bus was left on dry land as we, the disparate dozen, embarked on foot via a conventional gangplank. I use the word disparate as we were clearly a mixed and multi-national bunch. It seems as if I was the only Pom on the bus. Apart from Mr & Mrs Nip, there was a Chinese couple aged about thirty, a couple from Hobart, Tasmania, a couple from WA (Western Australia), two Asian chappies who could have come from anywhere between India and Indonesia, and a pleasant blonde lady called Anna from Botswana. And me. Plus Captain Kangaroo, our driver, guide and companion for the day. A baker's dozen of humanity.

A whistle was blown from somewhere and suddenly the huge bow ramp started to grind vertically upwards. The ship's hooter gave forth three sharp blasts to indicate she was going into reverse and we started to glide slowly out into open water. I was impressed to hear the international signal for 'I am going into reverse' as I would not normally have expected to bear witness to such maritime etiquette in this quiet backwater of Oz. In Sydney harbour, yes, but in a hot creek in Queensland? So far so good.

Although only seven-thirty in the morning, it was already hot and the sun was gliding upwards on its northerly trajectory. This was something that always confused me being in the southern hemisphere. I often wondered if it confused the earliest settlers and explorers too, with the tragic result of dying of thirst in a waterless, featureless bush. I made my way to the small but open cafeteria and bought a cold tin of beer and a large sausage roll which was pre-wrapped in a sort of plastic cling-film. I had never drunk beer so early in the morning.

One mouthful of the sausage roll was one mouthful too much. It was totally bland and tasteless. With hindsight I don't know why I bought it. A Yorkshire habit, I suppose, where pork sausage is made from proper pork and the pastry, is short and crispy. I removed the entire wrapper and decided that any close by fish could enjoy a treat. I chucked it into the sea about twenty feet out from the boat, which by now was doing about ten knots – probably its maximum speed. The sausage roll floated for about five seconds – then in a rush of moving water it suddenly vanished. I gawped and wondered. Whatever it was that had taken it, I hoped they enjoyed it more than I. That was the first and last sausage roll I ever bought in Australia.

I decided to take in some sun and fresh air on the open top deck, where about fifty other tourists were sitting, mostly Japanese to judge from the plethora of Canons, Nikons and the like strung around their necks. I gazed up at the mainmast where flew the Australian Merchant Marine ensign. Shock horror! It was flying upside down, which is a way of a vessel signalling to others that she is in distress. I decided to have a laugh and made my way to the wheelhouse at the forward end of the top deck. I knocked politely on the glazed door and a semi-uniformed officer who was smoking a fag noticed me. He slid the door open about a foot.

'Yih. Can I help you, mate?'

'Is this vessel in distress, Officer?'

'Certainly not. Why do you ask?'

I motioned for him to come out on deck and pointed to the mainmast. He gazed skyward, shielding his eyes from the fierce sun with one hand. He was not pleased.

'Thanks for pointing this out, mate. I'll attend to it straight away'. He went back to the wheelhouse and grabbed a microphone that was hanging from a nearby hook. The noise was deafening.

'Attention Charlie, attention Charlie! Report to the bridge immediately.'

Down at the forward end near the bow ramp a Popeye lookalike glanced backwards and upwards towards the wheelhouse.

A minute later and the Master was pointing to the offending inverted ensign.

'What the fxxx did you think you were doing? Sort it out. Now!'

To the amusement of every passenger, Charlie started to climb the mainmast to correct his error. The Japs instantly produced camcorders from pockets and handbags, and before you knew it the upper deck resembled a film set from *Mutiny on the Bounty*. 'Charlie' instantly became Charles Laughton, to be preserved forever on the PCs of residents from Okinawa to Osaka. He did well until he came to the last ten feet or so when he ran out of ladder and had to shin up a narrowing mast like a chimp collecting high fruit from a tree.

Somehow he managed to invert and retie the ensign without descending, and when he reached back down to deck level everyone burst into applause. He smiled appreciatively at everyone. Everyone that is except me. As he went to the ladder to return to the vehicle deck he made a beeline for me, paused momentarily by my right ear and whispered 'Pommy bastard!' I took it as a compliment.

Within an hour our 'barge' was nosing into a creek surrounded by mangroves at the head of which was the concrete landing slipway. We felt a scrunch as the steel bows met concrete and within seconds the ramp was lowered. The vehicles on board drove off and we, the disparate dozen, also walked off the ramp. Captain Kangaroo took charge.

'This is our vehicle over here. All aboard.'

I had never seen a vehicle quite like it. It was a cross between a small bus and a Hummer, with a high clearance between the ground and its twin rear axles. It was painted white, which I hoped would reflect some of the sun's heat. By now it was already high 30s Celsius and I was sweating like a dingo's crotch, some of which we hoped to see for real at some time during the day. Fraser Island was renowned for its dingos, with dreadful accounts of attacks on humans, and even babies being eaten alive. Jeez!

We all got aboard to find a single aisle down the middle with six single seats on each side.

'Seat belts must be secured all the time the vehicle is moving. That's a company rule. No exceptions. You'll soon see why. If anyone needs a comfort stop just shout and I'll stop, but there'll be no privacy mind as you must not leave the track. Understood?' He didn't elaborate.

Those of us that spoke English or Strine nodded in the affirmative. The Chinese and Nips looked impassive, but don't they always? Anna the Botswanan blonde was sat opposite to me on the other side of the aisle. In a semi guttural Afrikaans accent she whispered across to me:

'I think we're going to have an interesting day with our Captain Kangaroo don't you, Mark? He's a bit of a mystery man, isn't he? I wonder what his real name is. Maybe he's on the run, you know, like an escaped convict.'

It was fun and tongue-in-cheek banter. Anna was very pleasant company for the rest of the day and told me that she and her veterinary husband ran a game park in Botswana.

We all soon realised why secure seat belts were compulsory as Captain Kangaroo guided the bus up the steepest and roughest roads, although to call them roads was a gross overstatement. His commentary was almost continuous as we climbed ever higher and into dense forest, so dense in fact that you couldn't see into it more than a few metres because the trees were very close together. Kangaroo was obviously an expert botanist and forester, and told us that he had acquired his Park Ranger skills in California. Anna laughed and whispered again.

'I told you so – probably San Quentin!'

We descended to sea-level and drove at great speed northwards on an almost flat beach about fifty metres wide and eighty miles long if you believed that its name, Eighty Mile Beach, was realistic. We paused for a break close to the wreck of the *ss Maheno,* a small passenger liner that had broken her tow rope in a storm more than seventy years earlier. What was left of her superstructure was rusted almost beyond recognition, as countless Pacific storms had taken their toll of what was once a nice example of the Clydeside shipbuilding industry's expertise. Kangaroo's sense of humour was becoming more apparent.

'No swimming allowed here. The wreck is a breeding ground for tiger sharks, and they swim close inshore chasing rays into very shallow water. So stay out. Only last week a bloke from Tasmania ignored my advice and within two minutes he was attacked and shouted out 'I've lost a leg – the bastard!'

I bawled back, thinking about blood loss: 'Are you sure? Which one?'

'Dunno mate. They all look the same to me.'

In any event we all stayed out of the water although Mr Nip looked very unhappy and explained in broken English that he wanted a swim. Kangaroo cheered him up.

'We can all take a dip in Lake McKenzie later on, mate.'

Really, a lake on Fraser Island? This was news to me. There was a moment of light relief when an RAAF F111 bomber screamed down the beach at a very low altitude in a mock attack on the *Maheno* and thus us, too.

'That's a couple of the boys from Amberley having a bit of fun. That's a base near Brissie for you foreigners, by the way.' I already knew that, as I had been at school in Hong Kong with the sons of Amberley-based RAAF staff.

'Right, jump back in. Next stop is Ellies Creek.'

About twenty minutes later we arrived at a wide stream that flowed across the beach into the Pacific from higher ground in the west.

'We'll stop here for half an hour. The water is a hundred percent pure, so take the chance to fill your water bottles up. It tastes beaut. If you want to pee, do it well downstream so to speak. I needed a leak and some more water. Isn't nature confusing sometimes? I walked a few hundred metres up a narrow track and found a small wooden footbridge crossing the stream which was only about two metres across. It was just slightly too high to reach down to fill my one litre capacity plastic bottle which was by then almost empty. I took my trainers and socks off (well I am a Pom) and jumped down into the crystal clear water which had a golden sandy bottom. Big mistake! What had looked from above like depth of less than a metre was in fact almost two. The water immediately came up to my chin and I could barely touch the bottom. Within seconds I found myself some distance downstream and decided to get out as soon as I saw a gap in the vegetation. And then I saw it. A big sign read 'Beware Keelback snakes', with an artist's impression of one. I simply detest snakes, and I was out of that water before automatic bowel evacuation cut in. I walked barefoot back to the bridge retrieved my socks and trainers and sheepishly went back to the bus where Kangaroo was propped against a wheel arch, hand-rolling a fag. He looked at me like I was something the cat had just sicked up.

'Awright mate. Did you get some water?'

This guy's sense of humour was as dry as I was wet.

'I saw a sign warning folks about keelback snakes, so I beat a hasty retreat, so to speak.'

'Yeah they're harmless but the sign scares the shit out of Poms.'

We stopped for some lunch at a place called Eurong. It was a NAAFI type canteen where you queued for ages for poor quality tucker of salad, bread and cold meat. It seemed like every bus full of tourists on the Island rendezvoused there at the same time to keep catering arrangements to the bare minimum. However we're not talking hundreds here as the number of vehicles and people allowed on the island at the same time is strictly limited. It was a depressing line-up for depressing food in part of a hotel resort type complex, but why the heck anyone would want to stay overnight here was lost on me. At least I had the charming Anna for company, and we both looked forward to the promised swim in the afternoon. An hour later and we were on our way again.

'As we climb higher it gets cooler and the vegetation changes' announced Kangaroo. Some of the trees were simply huge, including turpentine trees which, it was explained to us, were the only trees in the world capable of absorbing salt into their structure and this rendering them almost immune to the ravages of sea water. This was the reason they had been used a century and a half earlier in the construction of both London Docks and the Suez Canal. The things you learn on the world's biggest sand dune, which is exactly what Fraser Island is, geologically speaking.

'And it might surprise you to learn that there is more fresh water in the lakes of Fraser Island than there is salt water in the whole of Sydney Harbour.' Now that was a real surprise. Mid-afternoon we pulled up at a rudimentary car park where a couple of other buses were already parked. I use the term 'car park' loosely. It was a piece of flattish ground about the size of two tennis courts.

'This is Lake McKenzie. We'll be here for an hour. There's a hut to get changed in if you fancy a dip. There's nothing in the water that will kill you – only a tiny rainbow-coloured fish that is a species unique to Lake McKenzie. The lake itself was about a hundred metre walk down a narrow path, and I felt uneasy as I saw a large goanna lizard well over a metre long run into the undergrowth. Ugh! I just hoped they were at the top of the food chain. Surely there couldn't be anything bigger than that on the island. Wrong. The lake itself was a revelation. It was almost circular and, I'm guessing, maybe five hundred metres across. The water looked incredible and was in layers of different shades of blue and turquoise as you got towards the centre and the deeper water.

'Be careful with your bags. Keep them close to you as dingos have a habit of snatching them. They are not nice, particularly if you get bitten. The only proper medical centre is at Hervey Bay, and it would need a chopper to get here first to airlift you out.'

I started to wonder what else there might be that was not nice. The problem with Australia is that much of its unique wildlife is designed to kill humans very quickly. Anna peeled off her outer clothes to reveal a blue bikini which showed her ample attributes off to perfection. She ran into the water across the narrow sandy beach and shallow-dived into the aquamarine liquid. It looked enchanting, and I took a couple of shots for her with her camera. For the folks back home, no doubt. I made do with a deep paddle as I didn't want to fanny around with my contact lenses. In any case I had had my fill of water earlier before the keelback snake scare.

Half an hour later we started to make our way back up the track to the bus but were halted by a Park Ranger holding a walkie talkie and speaking to someone else near the car park.

'Sorry folks. Often happens at this time of day. Matilda has decided to take her afternoon nap in the car park, and until she's persuaded to move we'll have to wait. No worries.'

Matilda was a five-metre-long carpet python. I kid you not. Thankfully I did not actually see Matilda, who was removed by Rangers within a few minutes. Ugh! Via many kilometres of track roads we finally got back to the point where we had disembarked the barge. The tide was way out and she was nowhere to be seen. After about a half-hour's wait she chugged into view, sporting her ensign the correct way up, I was pleased to see.

The tide seemed to come in very quickly, and the lanky mangrove roots were soon semi-submersed in water. This was certainly no place to get caught, I thought. It could no doubt be damned dangerous. This time Kangaroo drove us onto the barge and we soon set sail for the mainland about an hour away. Just before we got off the bus to check out the onboard cafeteria, Kangaroo told us a lot more about the wildlife on the Big Island.

'Apart from the tiger sharks out from the beach there are at least a dozen species of venomous snakes including Eastern tai-pans, Eastern browns, death adders and then of course there's the "salties" (salt water crocs) that have been known to venture this far south and....'

We all just looked at each other. He wasn't joking.

Kangaroo dropped us all off in the reverse order from collecting us: Chinks, Nips, Tassies and Sand Gropers (people from WA) all left until there was just myself and Anna. She got off at a hotel and pecked me on the cheek to say cheerio.

'Jew wanna sit down the front, Pom?' boomed out the voice from our mystery Captain. It was another ten minutes ride to my drop-off and he opened up.

'You said you were from Scarborough, mate. Where they play cricket?'

Scarborough's famous Cricket Festival was renowned the world over and been played at and visited by hundreds of Aussies over the decades. The late great Richie Benaud had been many times, indeed I had shared a drink or two with him in the bar of the Royal Hotel on more than one occasion.

Captain Kangaroo told me he had the best job in the whole world and said he wanted to do it forever. He worked four days on followed by four days off, which rotated his days and weekends nicely. Apart from that he told me nothing about himself. We reached my bus stop and he turned off the engine and got out of the driver's seat.

'Tell me honestly, mate. Did you enjoy today?'

I looked him straight in the eye and I told him this:

'Captain Kangaroo, when I'm in a nursing home and counting on one hand the most memorable days of my life then I promise you today's trip to Fraser Island with you as my guide will be amongst those five days.' I gave him ten bucks for a beer.

'Mate, you've just made my day by saying that to me. Most folks don't bother.'

He meant it too. We shook hands.

'My pleasure. I still didn't catch your real name, by the way.'

'No. I didn't tell you.'

THE PIER

There's something about piers. I like them. I have walked the length of many in several countries. Maybe it's the feeling of freedom that 'walking over water' gives you, like you're defying nature. They have come in all shapes and sizes. Some long, some short. Some made of wood, some made of iron. This one seemed to be a bit of both but I have to say it was very long. Very long indeed. It was the pier at Urangan, Queensland and sometimes called the Dayman Pier. I have no idea why. Maybe a bloke called Dayman designed it, who knows?

I had passed by it a few days earlier on a 'walkabout', and with time against me that day I had resolved to come back to explore it. I had got a lift from Pialba, where I was staying more or less to the Pier itself. It was hot and sunny as you might expect in Queensland in early February.

I paused to read a Notice that gave a brief and illustrated history of the pier itself and, just as important, the restoration project completed by the local Council. It was impressive. This might not be Blackpool or Southend Pier but in its own way it had a commercial history that bettered most. It was built to make money, not take money. There was no 'end of the pier' show, no wurlitzer, no 'what the butler saw' machine and no 'kiss me quick' hats. In fact there was a big fat bugger all.

The Notice informed me that the pier was built between 1913 and 1917 to facilitate the export of sugar, timber and coal. It was a poignant reminder that although the nation had sent the bulk of its young men to fight for the Empire ten thousand miles away, commercial life back home continued, indeed boomed. I pointed my nose towards the ocean end and started walking.

The tide was in and very soon, perhaps within a hundred metres or less, I found myself looking down over water. The railings were iron and looked a lot newer than the timbered floor beams. After my excursion to Fraser Island a few days earlier and my new knowledge of sea-water-resistant timbers, I wondered whether the original beams had themselves originated on the 'Big Island', as it was known. No matter, I was simply curious.

There were remarkably few people about, and a late-middle-aged couple passed me heading back in the direction of land. They nodded and said 'G'day' in the time honoured Aussie manner. I reciprocated, as you do when in Rome, or even Queensland. I felt almost a local. Looking ahead I could see some human shapes, possibly a couple of hundred metres away. They didn't seem to be moving and within about five minutes I had caught up to them. All three were 'indigenous' females, and all of them were holding fishing rods over the side. I have always enjoyed a spot of fishing myself and I was eager to see what they were trying to catch. I approached the lady nearest to me.

'Hi. Any luck?'

There was only silence. She didn't even lift her head, let alone say anything, so intense was her stare at the line which disappeared into the water about twenty feet below. Oh well, try one of the others, I thought. I walked about ten paces and leant against the railing, leaving a diplomatic metre or so between myself and the third lady.

'Hi. Hoping to catch something nice for tea?'

'Go away!' So I did. Sadly that was the only opportunity I had to try and converse with Aboriginals during my entire three week visit. I had always wanted to join the Diplomatic Corps, but the bastards wouldn't have me!

I kept walking until I reached the end of the pier, which the Notice had told me was just under a kilometre from the start point. That's about a thousand yards to us Poms or about half a nautical mile which makes a lot more sense. I was over water, after all. The end of the pier came as a bit of an anti-climax. There was just....well, nothing. Had it been Scarborough, Whitby or Weston-super- Mare there would have been at least one ice ream vendor. Had it been Brighton or Southend there would have been at least two with a hundred-year-old 'turf war', regular missing people reports, and a Coroner's office permanently on standby. I just couldn't believe how quiet it was and looking back towards land the three silent fisher-women were the only humanity twixt my position out in the Coral Sea and the dry land a kilometre away.

I stayed there for maybe half an hour taking in the view of the whole of Hervey Bay including Point Vernon way over in the west and from where I had commenced my 'Walk' a few days earlier. I wouldn't be in a hurry to do that again I can tell you. I headed back towards dry land, taking my time and just enjoying the vista. To my left I noticed a plane in the sky which was obviously making its approach to Hervey Bay Airport. What a sound investment that had been by the local Council that owned it. There were now direct jet flights to other major cities and not just the Qantaslink prop service to Brissie about two hundred kilometres to the south. No wonder the whole area was prospering and the population growing. Why live in the 'rat race' of Brisbane when you can live in the 'Bay'?

I passed the three ladies fishing and I saw a white plastic bucket with sea water and hopefully the fruits of their labour therein contained. I did notice they were now fishing from the other side of the pier so maybe the wind, tide or both had changed in the hour or so since I had seen them earlier. As always when you make a journey in reverse it seems to be quicker, goodness knows why. There were several bench type seats at the edge of a park area and I noticed the couple that I had passed on the pier. They recognised me and waved, seemingly keen to speak.

'Did you enjoy the walk?' the lady offered.

'Yes, very much, thanks. I like piers.'

'Yi, we do too, don't we?' the man said as he nodded to the lady,who was obviously his wife. She took up the mantle.

'You're not from round here, are you? England, I'd guess. Maybe North?'

'Yes, Yorkshire, but I don't think I speak English with a Yorkshire accent....'

'You mean like Geoffrey bloody Boycott!'

We all laughed. They seemed a fun pair, these two, so I thought I'd hang around a bit.

'Why don't you join us?'

They shuffled along to make room for me on the bench. They just didn't stop talking. They had retired to Hervey Bay after owning and managing a Post Office for over twenty years in some hot, dusty inland hicktown more or less in the middle of Queensland. And I thought that people like that only existed in the Tales of the Flying Doctor. After ten minutes I knew the names of their kids, grandkids, dogs and goldfish.

'What made you leave 'home' and come to the coast?' I asked. The man replied.

'The heat and the snakes, mostly, mate.' Well I could certainly empathise with both those motives.

'Yih, it was the heat mostly', the lady added, as if snakes were somehow OK.

I told them about the ladies fishing and my lack of success in the communications department.

'Yeah, Abos are like that mate. Best left alone if you ask me.'

'So is the fishing any good here generally?'

'It is yih, very good by all accounts. At weekends loads of folks fish from the pier. It's renowned for it.'

'Will they have been fishing for anything in particular, or just chancing their luck?'

A broad grin developed across his deeply-tanned face, and I wondered what was coming next.

'Whiting, mate. Almost certainly whiting.'

FREO

As a keen geographer, I had been familiar with the Port of Fremantle for decades, in fact since school days. It was thus high on my 'must see' list. Dad had told me a lot about Fremantle from his WW2 Navy days. I already knew that the port was named after Admiral Fremantle R.N., the Fremantle family being noble and long-serving officers of the Senior Service. In the Upper Barrakka gardens in Valletta, Malta there is even a stone memorial to the 'Admiral of the Blue' Fremantle.

So it was with great excitement that I set off once again into unknown territory by bus and then by train from Murray Street in Perth's CBD. It was hot. Too bloody hot. The half-hour ride was very pleasant indeed, passing through the City's southern suburbs, including the famous Peppermint Grove where wealthy mining magnates lived. The views of bays and yachts were never-ending. The train eventually trundled slowly over an iron bridge over the narrow entrance separating the Swan River from the Indian Ocean.

It had come as a surprise on my first visit to Perth to learn that the City was actually well-inland of the Indian Ocean and was sited almost at the head of the Swan River. The other surprise was that the Swan wasn't actually a river but more of a massive creek with scores of inlets going in all directions. Once you had sailed into the 'River' from the Indian Ocean there was mile after square mile of safe anchorage. Little wonder it was the main point of settlement for the first colonisers of the land that subsequently became what we know today as Western Australia, the biggest and per capita richest of Australia's six States.

Bing bong! ''This train termites here at Freo.'

He should have added Fremantle for the benefit of visitors instead of just using the vernacular. Never mind, I was almost bilingual by now.

We all got out and the first thing that surprised me was how dated everything looked. The station itself looked like something out of the thirties. That's because it was. I saw a kiosk that sold papers, tobacco and, I hoped, cold water.

'Sorry, we've just closed!'

The lady attendant pointed to a sign informing customers of the opening hours. In fact it hadn't just closed as she hadn't even pulled down the archaic-looking roller-blind that was operated by a hook at the end of a pole.

'We close at twelve on a Saturday.'

I didn't argue, there wasn't any point. Already I began to feel as if I was in a time warp in wartime Britain. I wouldn't have been surprised to hear an air raid siren go off. I would have to find somewhere else to buy some water. The litre I had brought with me had already proved pitifully inadequate and I had dumped the empty plastic bottle in a garbage bin. Sod the recycling. It was too hot to worry about that.

On exiting the station I noticed a large Victorian church to my left on exiting the station which was sited in its own capacious grounds. Crossing the main road and turning into Market Street it became immediately apparent that 'Freo' had retained many of its old buildings so characteristic of the colonial era. This lent it a certain charm so missing in 21st century Perth with its glitzy steel and concrete office towers fuelled and financed by the commodity boom. Perthites converted RMBs into skyscrapers and China turned iron ore into computers, cellphones and TVs and then sold them back to Perthites. No wonder they didn't make much in Australia any more. They'd be brewing Swan Lager on the Pearl River next. Don't laugh, it could happen.

I needed a drink, anything liquid and cold. I found a café soon enough and I was bemused by a printed notice on the door – 'No Abos, No Subos, No Retards.' As I said, it was like going back in a time machine. I bought two cold beers and a bottle of water to put in my bag and sat outside under a vacant umbrella. I got into conversation with two Swedish couples who initially thought that I was a local. They asked me directions to the old gaol which was now a tourist attraction. Fortunately I had studied a map before setting out and I was able to tell them how to get there and via which street. I asked them to return the favour by asking them to sing '*Waterloo*' for a laugh in praise of ABBA. To my utter amazement they did just that, well most of it anyway. Maybe they'd been asked to do it for a laugh on previous occasions. We got some strange looks from some-passers by I can tell you.

I moved on down Market Street and eventually turned right into High Street. I clocked a souvenir shop selling all manner of goods and made a mental note to stop in there on the way back. A few minutes later a gent seemingly in his seventies walked towards me and asked for a light. Protruding from a corner of his mouth was a small cigar. It was one of those that had a small white plastic mouthpiece like a miniature clarinet. I occasionally used to smoke one myself and I think they were called White Owl and were popular with American sailors. A US Navy mate called Don Ramsey who used to work at the PX in Hong Kong used to gift me the odd packet of six. Anyway, to continue the tale.

'You got a light, mate, for an old sailor?'

'Sorry, I don't smoke any more.'

'You're not from round here, are you?'

'No, I'm visiting from...'

'You got a light, mate, for an old sailor?'

It suddenly dawned on me that this chap was three sheets to the wind, if not four. I glanced upwards to see a sign that read 'naval club' or something similar. I don't think it was RSL as I would have remembered. I apologised and moved on, hoping he found someone to oblige him. He was quite harmless, just pissed. I walked the length of High Street and immediately spotted the Roundhouse, the Old Gaol, ahead of me. Like the ABBA wannabees, I also wanted to look inside, as I'd read a lot about it.

I was less than thirty-odd metres from the front gate when out of the blue, I kid you not, a bloody train passed right in front of me from left to right doing about twenty knots. It was most unnerving! Then I saw a sign that said 'Beware of Trains.' It was either the effect of the heat, the beer, or both. Next day's headlines in the *Western Australian* could so easily have read 'Pommy tourist minced by Freo train' or something equally unflattering. Anyway, shaken not stirred in Bond fashion, I proceeded to take a short tour of the old Gaol. A lady guide informed me it had originally been built to accommodate only eight prisoners, but that when more felons arrived from England they had to build a bigger one. She had a twinkle in her eye when she told me that. That's Aussie humour for you but when many Australians refer to Perth as a Pommy Ghetto, you can perhaps understand it.

I walked for a while and took in nice views of small harbours for fishing and pleasure boats. I couldn't help but notice the queue of large vessels waiting to berth in the Port itself. A helpful onlooker, obviously a local, told me that some of the ships rode at anchor for days, so fearful were they of 'missing their slot' to unload in what was Western Australia's only deep water port.

By mid-afternoon the heat was really getting to me and I decided to return to the train station by retracing my route. I couldn't believe it when the same 'old sailor', who was by now five sheets to the wind, asked me for a light again. Bless him.

I found the souvenir shop I had spotted earlier and spent a good fifteen minutes looking for a few bits to take back to England. After choosing several packs of black coasters with highly-decorated 'Abo' symbols inlaid into them I took them to the counter to pay for them, satisfied I had found something genuinely Australian. The young girl on the checkout was about sixteen, still a schoolgirl and quite chatty.

'Where do you come from? Mind me asking?'

'Not at all, I'm from Scarborough in Yorkshire.'

'Oh wow, my Grandad came from Yorkshire. A place called Hewell.'

'I think you might mean Hull.'

'No, Hewell, spelt H-U-L-L.' I just smiled, not wanting to correct her.

'These coasters are really nice, aren't they? Really Australian. You've just bought the last ones we have in stock. We're waiting for some more to come from China.'

ROTTO

I'd heard about Rottnest Island, not just from studying the geography of Australia at school, but from my father who'd been in the Royal Navy in Australia in WW2. Lying some 12 nautical miles almost due west of the Port of Fremantle, it had a strategic significance. Fremantle was the biggest submarine base in the armoury of the Allies fighting Japan. If the Imperial Japanese Navy attacked 'Freo', then they would have to get past the guns mounted on Rottnest Island first. It didn't happen, although there were many sightings of Japanese submarines. Today Rottnest Island is a 'must see' attraction for all tourists to Perth. The main reason for that is that there isn't much else.

So when my host, Lynne, announced that 'We're all going to Rotto tomorrow', I was quite excited. I have always liked islands, perhaps partly because I was born on one – Malta. For those amongst you (I suspect most Poms) who are not familiar with 'Strine', which is the Aussie equivalent of English, you have to understand that for a century or more Australians have bastardised the English language to make it easier to speak fewer and shorter words whilst remaining intelligible and understood. For the most part it works.

Examples are numerous and include 'draino', a cleansing fluid for drains in the vein of Jeyes fluid, the 'garbo' a dustbin man, and 'this arvo' meaning this afternoon. The suffix 'o' is omnipresent at the end of all these colourful words, which seem to roll off the tongue with ease. The above-mentioned Freo is yet another example and come to think of it, where did the word 'Abo' come from? It thus came as no surprise when my host Lynne announced one evening:

'Tomorrow, Mark , we're going to Rotto on a boat from Hillarys. We'll be leaving here at 'sparrows' and getting back sometime late arvo.'

Fortunately I was sufficiently bilingual by then not just to understand her but to wonder if she might slip some 'avos' (avocados) into our picnic lunch.

'Sparrows', or to give it its full title of 'sparrowfart', is an imprecise measurement of time in Australia. It usually means that time when the first hints of orangey daylight begin to appear in the east and when sparrows, allegedly, start to break wind. However in WA it is far more likely to be parrots or crows that are the first to shake a leg, so to speak. By then of course sparrows in NSW and Queensland, being two thousand miles further east, are almost ready for lunch. The measurement of time in Australia is perhaps another story for another day.

Suffice it to say that tomorrow arrived and the parrots and crows beat my alarm clock to it. The cats having been fed, we were on our merry way to Hillarys Boat Harbour by seven-thirty. Taking the same route as when we went to Sorrento Beach (the day of the Blueys), we arrived shortly after eight and met up with a large group of other folk who were also taking the same trip. It was a well-organised party and our names were read off and checked by some bloke who looked and sounded like a 'team leader.' Don't you just hate that title? I do. He looked and sounded like a teacher, so he probably was. He ran through some 'Rules' about this, that and the other like we were taking to the boats on the *Titanic* instead of going on a short jolly of about twelve miles or twenty kilometres to a metric Australian.

The boat was called the '*Aussie Warrior*' (can you believe that?) and was a pleasure craft designed to take about fifty people. There was plenty of shade if that's what you wanted, and with the formalities completed we departed the Harbour about nineish. We soon ran into a bit of a swell as we headed roughly west south-west towards our destination. You could make out Rotto as a brown lump on the horizon so the coxswain didn't have to use his satnav. It was already quite hot, and fortunately there was a bar on board and plenty of cooling ice, at least for the outward journey. Why there was little or no ice on the return journey will be revealed later. Always keen on the technical side of anything that floats, I asked the cox if he had an echo sounder onboard.

'Yip, here it is mate, look. The water is surprisingly shallow all the way to Rotto. No more than twenty metres most of the way. Lots of reefs too, mate, but no worries for us.'

I asked him why we were only doing about ten knots. Surely the '*Warrior*' could do twice that?'

'Oh yeah easily, mate but with this swell it would make the ride even rougher and some of the passengers might well, you know, get a bit green!' We both laughed and I mentally recalled the chorus line from one of Barry McKenzie's songs – '*We'll chunder in the deep blue sea!*'

Once we were a couple of miles out from the coast you had a decent view to landward and the distant skyscrapers of Perth's CBD were clearly visible through the heat haze. Likewise the only tall building at Scarborough Beach, which was called Observation City and financed by the well-known property magnate Alan Bond, the Pom with a predilection for porridge. I was enjoying every single minute of it and if anything was hoping for an increase in speed to make it a little livelier. Like my father once said to me:

'Tell you what, boy, you can't beat a bit of rough weather to cut down the queue at the bar!'

How right he was, and it is always something that I bear in mind on my regular crossings from Hull to Zeebrugge in Belgium.

It was probably mid-morning when the *Aussie Warrior* dropped anchor and one of the crew announced that the snorkelling was very good in this aquatic neck of the woods. Apparently it was called Geordie Bay. I was tempted to whistle 'The Blaydon Races' but thought better of it. Nobody would know what it was. Well, to be honest, the water didn't look to be very good to me but perhaps swimming in the gin -ike waters of the Maltese Archipelago as a kid had spoilt me, not to mention the warm clear waters of the Turkish Aegean. The boat's echo sounder told us we were in only five metres of water and you couldn't even see the bottom. Bugger that I'll have another beer.

Quite apart from that, I was absolutely terrified of the possibility of sharks. This was Western Australia after all, where swimmers and surfies were regularly on the lunch menu for tiger sharks and great whites. The incident with the 'blueys', although a false alarm, had already almost caused at least single incontinence, and I had no wish to repeat the experience. No, I would keep my powder, not to mention my shorts, dry and save my energy for a spot of land exploration. I had no idea what was coming. An hour later, and and all the Hans and Lotte Hass wannabees back on board the *Warrior,* we weighed anchor and sailed about a mile to the west to a place called Parakeet Bay. I must say, the waters looked a lot clearer here. Perhaps it was more sheltered and the wind and ocean swells didn't whip up the sandy bottom as much as in Geordieland. That was the trouble with WA as a whole. It was built on sand and under that was limestone. One of the crew took charge of a landing party, and a small rhib boat about four metres long with an outboard Yamaha engine was winched over the side.

'Right, which of you lot want to go ashore for an hour or two? Hands up!'

About eight hands reached skywards, including mine.

'OK tell you what, I'll take the first half of you ashore here, then I'll come back and take the rest to Little Parakeet Bay just round the promontory. I got in the first load, not concerned as to the size of the parakeet I was to visit. We were only about two hundred metres out from the beach, so within a couple of minutes the boat boy cut the engine and we glided onto the soft sand. Out we climbed. My first steps on Rotto! All I had to do now was keep my eyes skinned for a quokka, a miniature marsupial found only on Rottnest Island. My curiosity had been aroused when a week earlier I had noticed that a 'buy and sell' magazine delivered free to most Perth households was called 'The Quokka' and Lynne had put me right.

Lynne had stayed on the *Warrior* for some reason, but I had three other females for company, all probably in their thirties and all good fun. The boat boy had said he would come back for us at a certain time and take us round to join the others at Little Parakeet Bay. Time went by, and by, and by. Eventually we saw the rhib leaving the Warrior but to our horror it didn't head in our direction. It headed off towards the other bay of the same but lesser name. It never came back. This was bad news. Had he forgotten us? One of the girls suggested two alternatives.

'I reckon the bastard's forgotten, or this is a bad joke. We'll either have to swim round or climb up these dunes to the top. Hopefully we'll find a path to the other bay. There's bound to be one.'

There was nothing 'bound to' about this situation at all. The swim would be about a kilometre and after my 'blueys' experience was a complete no-no. In any case I had a small knapsack with a few bits and bobs in it, including a tin of by-now warm beer. As Otis Clay once sang – '*The only way is up, baby.*' I looked up at the dunes. Shit. To an average Pom a sand dune, like those at Southport or St. Andrews Royal & Ancient Golf Club, is about two metres high. I had walked in the Saudi desert west of Riyadh up huge dunes but these in front of us were something else. They must have been at least twenty metres high and very, very steep. One of the girls who was very slight of stature volunteered to go first. She seemed to have the right 'thrust to weight' ratio as it were, and only a couple of times did she start to slide back, but soon regained her composure and balance. She reached the top after a few minutes, disappeared and then reappeared a minute later.

'No worries! There is a path up going the right way, too. Who's next?'

'Both the other girls were obviously not on the F-Plan diet and I watched transfixed as they sat off upwards. They both got about half-way when they started to slide back at quite an alarming rate. The sand was red-hot in the mid-day sun, too, and really hurt their hands. They were both wearing thongs (flip flops to us Poms, not lingerie) which made matters worse as they acted like miniature skis. The girl at the top shouted down.

'Take yer thongs off and dig your toes into the sand.'

So they did, and the sand was cooler a couple of inches beneath the surface, too. Slowly but surely they inched their way up. It probably took them about ten minutes and they arrived at the top breathless but happy. Now it was my turn. They stared down to watch the overfed 'Sunburnt Pom' emulate a cross between a sand beetle and Edmund Hillary. I got almost halfway before I seemed to find myself in sand so loose I felt like a single grain heading for the narrow neck of an egg timer.

It was too late to take my trainers off, and in any case pirouetting on one leg whilst undoing laces was just too terrible to contemplate. Just staying calm was difficult, the drop to the sand and rocks below growing greater of course with every metre of dune scaled. I must have looked quite absurd as I moved one hand and one foot at a time, always keeping two of one and one of the other in the sand for grip. At least it was working, albeit painfully slowly, but what was the alternative? A heavy landing on the rocks below would bring severe injury, and that's looking on the bright side. For the first time in my life I was really scared.

'Come on, Mark, you can do it!' the girls screamed down. I could too, but only just. It must have taken fully fifteen minutes to reach the top. I swear to you, I have not had a boiled egg or used an egg timer since.

We followed the path to Little Parakeet Bay where others and the rhib were waiting. I gave the sheepish-looking boat boy a gobful of Anglo-Saxon. He wouldn't be getting a bloody tip later that's for sure. The rhib was beached half-in and half-out of the water, and one by one we got in until there was only one person, a fat lady, left. She was English and about fifty and about a hundred and twenty kilos. In the words of the National Express song 'her arse was the size of a small country', and the boat boy was keen to ensure that her bulk did not disrupt the balance of the boat as she boarded.

'Do not put one foot in first and then step in. It's very slippery. Put your er....backside on the inflated side, then swivel your legs in at the same time.'

So what did this dumb broad do? She put one foot in first, then as she transferred her considerable weight from shore to ship she inevitably went 'tango utopia' and her entire arse, which alone probably weighed in at thirty kilos, slammed down onto my right foot. I heard something crack, unsure if it was bone or part of the boat. Instantly I was in agony. Five minutes later and back on the Aussie Warrior, the coxswain, who doubled up as first aider, peeled off my trainer. My foot was already starting to swell. And that folks is why there was no ice for cold drinks on the journey back to Hillarys. My right foot was immersed in a bucket of the stuff all the way.

There was one last highlight to remember as if two weren't already enough. About half-way back we passed a small cabin cruiser that was burning quite fiercely, and another bigger vessel standing by which seemed to have lifted off the passengers to safety. I asked the cox what Search and Rescue services were like, assuming that as in the UK it would be the Coast Guards or the Royal Australian Air Force.

'Will the RAAF be coming from Pearce?' which was an Oz Air Force base not too far away.

'No, mate. It was privatised recently. It's now commercially sponsored by a bank.' I was stunned.

'You must be joking! A bank?'

'Yep, I know. It's a bloody disgrace mate, if you ask me. There's a bloody Air Force base to the north and a bloody great Navy base at Garden Island just to the south of here.'

'So where does the chopper, if it ever arrives, actually come from?'

'I have absolutely no bloody idea mate. Honest.'

'So how long do you think it might take, assuming one is coming?'

'Dunno, mate. If the pilot's gone to the cricket, maybe later rather than sooner.'

Like I said in an earlier story, WA stands for Wait Awhile.'

FOUR HOURS OF MAMBA

My stay in Brisbane, Queensland's State Capital, had been short and sweet. The day of my departure had arrived and my hosts, Keith and Sushma Griffin, took me back to the city's airport known as Eagle Farm and we said our goodbyes. It might be a year or more before we would meet again, probably back in Yorkshire where Keith's father Harry still lived. Unusually for a professional pilot, Keith had a habit of always cutting it fine time-wise and we screeched to a halt outside 'Departures' with the narrowest margin of time left to check in. Keith looked at his watch.

'Plenty of time, I told you.' You could have kidded me. That's an ex-Phantom pilot for you!

I checked in the 22kg suitcase at the Domestic Qantas desk and the clerk raised a quizzical eyebrow as if to indicate that I was slightly over the baggage allowance. I was just about to tell her that I had lost at least two kilos of sweat two days earlier on Fraser Island when she looked up, smiled and said:

'No worries. Enjoy the flight, Sir.'

I made my way through to the departure lounge and the multitude of shops selling 'Australiana' and other tat like plastic Jumbo jets with a red 'Flying Roo' on the tailplane. One shop that did interest me though was one selling honey of several different types. My neighbour in England, Barbara, is very partial to honey and as I was only to spend a few more days in Perth WA before the long hop back to Blighty I decided to buy some for her. I selected a large jar labelled Best Queensland Clover Honey and took it to the checkout to pay for it. The assistant asked for my Boarding Card which was sticking out of my pilot style shirt breast pocket.

'I'm sorry, Sir, but you're not allowed to buy this honey. It's against the law.'

Now, if I was buying a high velocity rifle with a hundred rounds of ammo or enough semtex to create a new Kalgoorlie gold mine I could have understood it. But honey?

'You're flying to WA, Sir correct? My boarding card did not lie. Yes, I was indeed flying non-stop to Perth.

Is that a problem, Miss?'

'Sorry, regulations state that you're not allowed to take honey out of the State of Queensland and as you're flying to WA I'm afraid I'm not allowed to sell it to you.'

She gingerly picked up the offending jar and placed it on a lower and out-of-sight shelf like it was some kind of unexploded bomb. I was perplexed.

'Can't we just pretend I'm flying to Cairns, you know just between me and you?'

'No sorry, Sir. It's all to do with preventing the spread of diseases that affect the bees here in Queensland. See?' No I didn't see at all.

'So is there a sign every so often along the State border with New South Wales that tells bees not to cross the line but to turn back to the Gold Coast?' She giggled a girly laugh.

'I see what you mean.'

I explained to her that it was a pressie for my neighbour in England.

'Tell you what then, you can buy some WA honey at Perth Airport when you leave Australia. No worries.'

In the circumstances that seemed like very good advice which I would act upon a week later. But that's another story for another day.

'Bing bong!'

'Qantas announce departure of Flight QF blah blah blah departing from Gate number etc.'

There were only about a hundred passengers ready assembled at the Gate to board the Boeing 767. Now I don't know about you but I always look at my fellow travellers and try to pre-judge who I would not like to be sitting next to. It is probably not very sociable but that's just me. There was diversity of ages and sexes as you might imagine. One bloke stuck out from the rest. He was about six foot tall, five feet across and wore a khaki coloured safari suit. Aged in his late sixties and unshaven he looked like a hybrid of David Bellamy, the world renowned botanist, and David Attenborough, the knighted and much acclaimed zoologist. His rucksack was huge and bulging with God knows what. He would have difficulty in getting that into the overhead locker that's for sure. Let's hope there weren't any bees in it trying to cross the State line. He looked like a 'voted off' reject from *I'm a celebrity get me out of here*' the phoney reality TV show that is so popular in UK with armchair naturalists, the location set of which was not too far away.

I boarded the plane and made my way to row number whatever as directed by the Qantas hostie wearing one of those 'Abo type' uniforms that makes them look like a heap of lizards' entrails. I'd requested a window seat in front of the wing to get an unobstructed view. Flying across the outback across the whole of Australia non-stop and in daylight had been an ambition for many years. I just wanted to gaze down at three million square miles of *Ten Town*, *The Flying Doctor* and *Walkabout,* the last a movie that had made a huge impression on me as a teenager, an amazing forty years earlier. True, I wouldn't be able to spot Jenny Agutter from thirty thousand feet, but at least I could pretend.

'I'm sorry, Sir, but you can't put that rucksack in the locker. It's too heavy. It should have been checked in as hold baggage.'

The conversation was getting closer to me by the second. Oh no! 'Bellaborough' was heading for my row and the two vacant seats to my left. What bad luck. He looked as if he hadn't had a Tyrone Power for days and probably stank like a skunk, or whatever the Oz equivalent is. The hostie saved my bacon.

'Take the aisle seat please, Sir, to give the gentleman by the window more room and leave the middle one free.' She was obviously a trained diplomatic. What she should have said was:

'You fat freak you look and smell as if you've been in the bush for weeks. You should have gone in the hold never mind your rucksack.'

The lady was a Qantas charm school graduate for sure. Bellaborough did not look happy and before a male steward carried the offending baggage to the rear of the aircraft which was less than half full, he removed a large book from the outer zippered pocket and stuck it in the pouch containing the Qantas magazine, the escape manual for a 767 miraculously landing upright on the sea or Lake Torrens and the regulatory puke bag. Two more hosties did the familiar lifejacket stand up comedy routine despite the fact we would never see the sea during the five hour flight. Maybe they were normally on the Auckland route across the Tasman and did the show out of habit. The aircraft pushed back with a slight jerk and the cabin lights flickered as the APU was replaced by the main engines – two massive General Electric turbofans in this case. Bing bong!

'G'day this is your Captain speaking. We will shortly be departing for our non-stop flight to Perth WA. Our route today will be following a slightly different course than normal thanks to a strong westerly jetstream. We'll be taking a more southerly route and flying at a lower altitude than normal to minimise the effects of the headwind. Our First Officer will be giving you further updates during the flight but in the meantime, just sit back and enjoy the flight.' Bing bong.

Good, a lower altitude eh? That might mean I could see a bit more on the ground. Who knows? What is there to see exactly? I decided to ask Bellaborough. Could be he was a frequent flyer on this route. I turned sideways intending to ask him but at once I could see he was engrossed in his book which looked like a 'Guide to Australian moths' so I didn't bother him. We took off and headed almost due west for a while then banked to the south as the Captain had intimated. I looked down at Brisbane's CBD and promised myself to return for a longer visit next time. Passing the city the land looked lush and green as we passed over the outer suburbs of Indooroopilly, Chelmer and then as we gained height a town I thought might have been Ipswich. Within a few more minutes we turned rightish and the sun was shining brilliantly and bouncing off the wing like a laser through the cabin windows. I reached for my Polaroid sunnies and kept staring out of the window. Bellaborough started to look agitated and gestured for me to slide down the blind. No way mate! I had waited years to see this and I didn't want to miss any of the sights below us. There were plenty of empty seats on the other side unaffected by the sun and he could bloody well move if he and his moths weren't happy.

Slowly but surely the lush green vista below turned brown then orange then red. This is what I wanted to see. The so-called Red Centre. The hosties brought us coffees and snacks and Bellaborough stopped reading for a few minutes but didn't even look in my direction, let alone speak, despite the fact that we were both sharing the pop-down shelf on the unused centre seat. Bing bong!

'G'day, this is your First Officer speaking. We're flying at about only six thousand metres today due to the weather conditions but this means you'll be able to see more and I'll point out some interesting sights as we progress. We have just passed over the State line into New South Wales.'

I looked down wondering if I could see some bees doing a U turn. I wondered what feature, if any, marked the State border or was it just a straight line on a map for the convenience of cartographers?

Our helpful co-pilot made several more announcements over the next half hour pointing out in turn an irrigated farm (wow) a north-south Highway named after a famous explorer – so famous I can't remember his name – an opal mine and finally a dried up soda lake. So much for the life vest drill!

He was not giving up this guy.

'Anyway, that's about it for a while and as we have got about four hours of mamba coming up I'll give you another shout as we're coming in to WA.' Bing!

Mamba? I decided to make one last effort to speak with Bellaborough. I spoke loudly so he couldn't help but hear me.

'Excuse me. What is mamba please?'

His weather-beaten face turned through ninety degrees towards me and he mumbled the only six words he spoke to me in the entire five hour flight.

'Miles and miles of bugger all.'

WE DON'T TIP IN AUSTRALIA

I had just flown into Brisbane Airport on the QantasLink flight from Hervey Bay, a short hop of about forty-five minutes. The twin-prop Dash 8 was bang on time and it was early evening, with the tropical light just starting to fade. I claimed my trusty Delsey suitcase from the carousel and made my way outside looking for the taxi rank. I soon spotted a queue of similarly-minded folk, but what surprised me was that they were being marshalled into order by a Sikh chappie wearing an orange jumpsuit and a yellow turban. Without the turban he could have been one of those residents of Camp X-Ray and a guest of Uncle Sam at Guantanamo Bay in Cuba. He seemed terribly efficient and was directing people and their baggage to various waiting areas. Then it was my turn.

'Where to? Where do you want to go?'

'Into the CBD, please, Wyndham Terrace I think.'

'You think?'

'The United Services Club, Wyndham Terrace.'

'Bay number 2. Wait there.'

He pointed to a white line, but I couldn't see any number painted anywhere. A big yellow cab suddenly arrived and the driver, who looked like he was a pensioner of many years' standing, got out.

'Where to, mate? Is that your only bag?' he asked, pointing to my one case. A smaller knapsack I carried separately, and as it contained my passport, money, ID, a Telstra cellphone, tickets and everything important, I was always reluctant to let go of it. The driver opened the boot to reveal a disappointingly small capacity as it was largely occupied by a massive tank containing LPG. I was quite taken aback. What if I'd had a wife, two kids and four cases? Where on earth would they all be stored? My sole case only just fitted in, and the driver slammed the lid shut and jumped back into his seat. I got in the back seat as normal. Big mistake.

'I have had a shower today, mate.'

'Sorry?'

'You can sit in the front, mate. You must be a Pom. Poms always like sitting in the back. Get in the front, mate, and we'll have a banter.'

So I did. After establishing where I wanted to go, he seemed quite surprised.

'No wonder you're all spivved up, mate. It's quite a posh place. Are you a member?'

I explained that I was meeting my old mate Keith who was in the process of applying for membership,being ex-RAF. Tonight was an official invitation together with his wife to meet Club officials, presumably to see if they were 'suitable' membership material. I thought this was most odd in egalitarian Australia and that it sounded more like some hidebound gentlemen's club in Mayfair, London, than a colonial-style ex-servicemens' watering hole.

The cabby's name was Arthur Clark, and I jokingly asked him if his middle name began with a 'C' to emulate the scientist renowned for his off-the-wall fantasies – most of which were coming true. He just laughed.

'So you're dining there as well tonight, mate? I've heard the food and the service are very good. Just as well you knew about the dress rules.'

I told Arthur that a text message from Keith a couple of hours before I had left Hervey Bay had warned me to wear a clean shirt, jacket and tie. As if I had that sort of kit with me on holiday in Australia in February! Cousin Paul had come to the rescue with his own ex-RAF tie with half a silver wing embroidered on it, a neat white 'Made in Australia' Monogram white shirt and a smart navy-blue Marks & Spencer blazer bought in London on his last visit to the Old Country. Overindulging in both food and drink run in the family genes, so they both fitted to perfection. How fortunate.

It was quite a long ride into the City and Arthur took the opportunity to educate me on a variety of topics. He told me he was in his mid-seventies and had no intention of retiring as long as he could still obtain his licence. He told me that his family originally came from Ipswich, Suffolk, and that by coincidence he now lived 'out on the Ipswich Road' to the south-west of the City. He told me how much Australia, and Queensland in particular, had changed over the last fifty years.

'And not much for the better I can tell you, mate. There's far too many bloody foreigners from all over coming here to Queensland. Half of bloody China seems to live on the Gold Coast, mate. You bccn there yet?'

'Er no, I haven't, but if I have time I've an old mate who now lives near a place called Burleigh Waters. I might visit him.'

'Yih, well take my advice, mate. Half the hookers in Asia have moved in there. Best to keep your own snake in your own pants, if you know what I mean, mate?' We both laughed.

'So that must mean that Queensland is booming then, Arthur? You know, financially. Sex usually follows the money.'

'Oh yih. Queensland and WA are the only two States that are getting richer. WA because of the mining and sky-high mineral prices, and Queensland....'

'Because of the Asian fanny!' We both laughed out loud again. I liked this guy, a real character. Commodity prices apart, he was a mine of information. Excuse the pun. I decided to tap him up for tips on what to see and where to go on my next visit to Brisbane which I would ensure was a lot longer even if I did have to wait a year or two.

'Well, the Castlemaine Four X Brewery is a must-visit, mate. It's a virtual beer-making museum now and only a matter of time before it moves into one of those plastic and steel, robot-controlled places making beer that is fit only for Poms to drink.' He glanced sideways and winked. I was half- minded to tell him that some of England's finest ales are brewed in Suffolk by Adnams.

'Oh yih, and make sure you go on a river cruise on one of those paddle boat steamer things. They chuck in lunch as well. The Moreton Bay bugs are particularly nice.'

I decided not to ask what they were. It sounded to me like a 'bush tucker trial' on that jungle reality TV show to me.

'So, Arthur, apart from Chinese and Poms, who form the bulk of visitors to Queensland? Kiwis?'

'No way, mate, no way. I'd say Japs beyond a shadow of a doubt. I don't mind 'em. Mind you, I wasn't in the War. Actually if they had invaded Australia in 1944 then word has it they were gonna chuck all the Abos in the sea. So they would have done some good.' I waited for the sideways wink. It never came.

We were now not far from the City centre. Eventually we pulled up outside a colonial, military-style colonnaded building that looked liked something out of Kipling.

'Here we are, mate, this is it. Looks like you're expected. Look!'

A steward sporting a white tunic with lots of brass buttons was already half way down the steps.

'Are you Mr Harland?' I nodded and stifled a grin. I wasn't sure if this was a prank of Keith's or real. He took my very heavy suitcase and carried it up the steps to the glazed front door. Arthur looked bemused.

'Well I've bloody seen it all now. First time here and some servant wants to treat you like Royalty. No wonder you wanted to sit in the back mate.' He was only pulling my leg.

'How much do I owe you, Arthur?'

'Oh tell you what, call it thirty bucks.' I peeled off two yellow twenty dollar bills and handed them to him.

'Have a beer on me, Arthur, and thanks for the chat.'

'We don't tip in Australia, mate.'

'Then you're bloody lucky I'm a Pom, aren't you?'

This time the wink did arrive.

CESSATION OF HOSTILITIES

The young bartender in my hotel, The Ibis on Turbot Street, had recommended that I take a trip on a paddle steamer on the Brisbane River. I had been in 'Brissie', the state capital of Queensland, for a couple of days, had already walked around large chunks of that lovely city, and was open to suggestions. The young chap's name was Matthew, and he was extremely polite and helpful.

'You can get a better view of the city from the river than anywhere else. Trust me.' So I did. On an earlier short stopover in Brisbane a taxi driver, Arthur, had made the same recommendation.

I pre-booked a ticket on the Kookaburra River Queen the day before to make sure. The city was still busy with Australia Day holidaymakers, and I didn't want to miss out. The ticket price included an 'eat as much as you like' seafood buffet which suited me down to the ground. I boarded the boat near the centre of the CBD and I was immediately surprised, not at how full it was, but at how many of my fellow passengers were obviously Asian. Now I can't speak either Chinese or Japanese much beyond 'two beers please' or 'good morning', but unlike Sydney, which resembles downtown Peking, (I refuse to call it 'Bay Jing') Brissie, if anything, on that day resembled Kyoto. Only the cherry blossoms were missing. It reminded me of that old joke – 'If there's a chink in the curtain and a nip in the air then you know you're in the Far East.' Political correctness has never been my thing.

There were Japanese tourists all over the boat. Not much chance of chatting to an Okker Oz today I thought to myself. I was wrong. However, the last person to board was an elderly chap, obviously local, and it seemed to me as if the boat had been waiting for him. He actually arrived on a push-bike, dismounted, and wheeled his bike up the gangplank. It was surreal. He exchanged a few words with a crew member who welcomed him aboard.

'G'day Col, 'ower yer goin, mate?'

'Awright, mate. Are we ready for off now, mate?'

Good God – don't tell me this bloke was crew?

As Matthew the bartender had told me, the views of the city skyline were terrific. For those of you who have never visited Brisbane, a river cruise is a 'must do.' From the air the broad river looks like a huge brown python making its way from the inland suburbs of Chelmer and Indooroopilly through the centre of the city itself before hitting the Pacific Ocean in Moreton Bay. Bearings are easy to establish from the air. However, on the water the visitor can be excused for losing his or her sense of direction every few minutes, such are the twists and turns the boat takes to navigate the river and its many bridges. There was an on-board commentary from time to time coming over the speakers.

'On your left is the old City Hall built in etc. etc. and in a few minutes we'll be passing under the Goodwill Bridge, the most recently built in Brisbane to span the river....and on your right is the Queensland Maritime Museum which boasts many exhibits from the early colonial days, the Second World War and right through to the present day...'

It was all very interesting, but being a foodie, my ears pricked up a tad when the male's voice was replaced by a female's announcing the procedure for accessing the buffet lunch which was about to be served.

'Lunch is now being served according to your seat number. Those in seat number from one to twenty (or whatever) can go for their buffet now, please.'

I had no idea I was even sitting in a numbered seat! Eventually I discovered one somewhere and my heart sank. My number was fifty something! By the time it came to my turn there would probably just be scraps left. Now Japanese folk being what they are anything that comes from the sea is fair game on a plate, whether it be squid, dolphin, minke whale or sushi at a zillion yen a gobfull.

Suddenly there was a major kerfuffle at the rear of the boat as it seemed that every occupant of seats one to twenty came from between Okinawa and Osaka. My suspicions were confirmed. There would just be squid's arse'oles left when it came to my turn. Suddenly my attention was diverted by a tap on the shoulder and a friendly voice. It was 'Col', the bloke with the bike.

'Greedy bastards those nips, mate. If they didn't spend loadsa money we wouldn't have 'em here. Colin. What's your name mate?' He stuck his hand out to shake mine.

'Mark, hi. I saw you come aboard with your bike. You're still working then, Col, you must be a veteran now surely?'

'Yeah mate, late seventies but it keeps me going. A bit of beer money. Your first trip to Brissie?'

'Second, actually, but I didn't see much first time round so I thought I'd come back. Dad was here during the War on a destroyer chasing Japanese submarines. His brother Bernard was also here on the carrier HMS *Unicorn* at the Battle of Leyte Gulf.' Col's ears pricked up.

'Was he now, mate? In that case you'll be interested in visiting the Maritime Museum I mentioned earlier. It's over there. Look!'

He pointed to an area that seemed to be half-way under the Goodwill Bridge. What did he mean by 'mentioned earlier.' Suddenly it dawned on me. Col was the commentator over the microphone! He continued.

'In that big dry dock is the frigate HMAS *Diamantina,* which was named after a river here in Queensland. Very few people are aware of this, but the final surrender of all Japanese Forces in the Pacific was signed on the deck of the *Diamantina.* The Septics and history tell you it was all done on the *Missouri* in Tokyo Bay, but I'm telling you it wasn't, mate. That was just for the cameras. That's the reason we preserved the *Diamantina.* Go take a look for yourself, Mark. Crikey, we're almost at Cooks Bridge. I'd better shake a leg. I'm back on duty on the mike.'

I wondered what was left to say by way of commentary, as I knew we were about to 'chuck a uey' and head back up river. A few minutes later as we were passing the Museum on our left Col's voice came over the mike.

'On the port side is the World War Two preserved warship the *Diamantina,* on which the final surrender of all Imperial Japanese forces was signed. A coupla years ago two smart-arsed bastards from Canberra with fancy suits and briefcases came up saying they wanted to change the wording of the commemorative plaque on board from 'surrender' to 'cessation of hostilities.' Well, I'm telling you now. It was not cessation of hostilities. It was a total bloody surrender. Bloody right, mate.'

They don't make Aussies like Col any more. That's all I'm saying. If he's still there on my next trip, I'll buy him a beer. Or three.

ROSEBERY WHERE?

Chelmer. It was only a one stop ride on the train from the place with the crazy name – Indooroopilly. Pronounced 'Indropilli' to make it easier for Poms, like me. Both were suburbs of Brisbane on on the main railway line to Ipswich. I was taking a trip out from the city to see my old friends Keith & Sushma Griffin who lived in Chelmer so I took the train from Roma Street Station (that's Brisbane's equivalent of Kings Cross to fellow Poms). The trains were not all that frequent and were still not back on their normal schedule after Australia Day. It meant I had time to spare so I decided to alight at 'Indropilly' and go walkabout for an hour or two. I had been there once before with Keith two years earlier and he had parked his car in a shopping complex. Eventually I found it not too far from the train station and decided it was time for a coffee and a snack. The café occupied a big open area and was surrounded by shops selling all manner of consumer goods. I spotted a shop selling every kind of greetings card and I remembered buying a Valentines card there two years ago to present to my host Lynne in Perth to where I was flying that afternoon. On this occasion I bought some postcards to send to the God daughters in Scarborough and decided to write them while I sat in the café. I went to the kiosk as it was obviously self-service and ordered a 'long black' which is Ozspeak for a large black coffee.

'Would Jew like a blueberry muffin to go with that?' said the young female attendant.

Now quite why muffins have crept into the café society of both Australia and England I have no idea. American in origin, perhaps they were invented to remind people of the bulge above their belts. Sadly England and Australia were going the same way. And no, I didn't want a bloody muffin filled with anything, let alone a fruit that would stain my shirt with the first squirt.

'Do you have anything that is Australian? I'm just a visitor.'

'Yi, how about a nice lamington. Jew like coconut?'

I did indeed so that's what I settled for, a lamington. I had been in Australia just long enough to learn that a lamington was a chocolate cake covered in desiccated coconut. Whether there was ever a Mr or a Mrs Lamington who dreamt that one up I don't know. Australia had been the origin of quite a number of unique sweet dishes and Pavlovas and Melbas sprung to mind. In any event there was definitely no lamb involved which was a disappointment to me as a lover of kebabs and chops. No worries. I took my plate and cup of coffee to a spare seat, took out a pen from my small knapsack and started writing.

'Dear Lucy, as I write this I am munching on a lamington … etc.'

That would cause a squeal when it arrived back in Yorkshire as I knew young Lucy was very animal friendly. I could hear from ten thousand miles away.

'Dad, Uncle Mark's eating a lamb in a café in Australia! Disgusting!'

I had made a point a point of posting a card to Lucy and her sister Millie from every major place I visited in Australia, even Tasmania. I wrote the cards for which I already had postage stamps and popped them into a letterbox. I would not be back in Yorkshire for two weeks, time aplenty for them to reach their destination before I returned myself. Some hope. Replenished with coffee and lambless cake I exited the shopping mall and made my way to the train station taking care to board the train heading to Chelmer and not one heading back to Brisbane.

Having phoned the Griffin household earlier on my recently purchased prepaid Telstra cellphone I was disappointed to discover that Keith would not be there. A semi-retired pilot he had taken a chartered A330 'up north' for a few days. Sushma had told me to come and have some supper with her and the boys, Jeremy & Elliot.

'Call me when your train gets into Chelmer. I'll come and pick you up, Mark.'

'Thanks, Sush, but I like a walk. I'm sure I can remember the way. See you later.'

Big mistake. On getting off the train I should have crossed the bridge to the other side of the track before taking my bearings. I didn't. As a consequence I started walking in completely the wrong direction. I didn't recognise any landmarks I was looking out for. Not that there ever are many landmarks in the suburbs of Australia's major cities. In England it would be a case of 'turn right at the Red Lion, carry on till you reach the church on your left, turn right at the White Hart and once you've passed the Crown Tavern it's the second on your left.' You get my drift. Well there's none of that lark in Oz. There are one of two things. Either miles and miles of bungalows or miles and miles of bugger all. Right then I was faced with the latter. A dipping sun told me I was heading west, that was for sure. I was following a path of some sort but it just seemed to lead to nowhere, just more grass and scrub.

Suddenly, out of the blue, I spotted a push-bike about a hundred metres ahead coming full pelt towards me. The rider was helmeted, head down and doing a substantial rate of knots. I would feel a bit of a tosser but I felt I had no option but to try and stop him to ask directions. I stood my ground in the middle of the path and held my hands up like a surrendering soldier, hoping he would stop. When he was about twenty metres out he still showed no signs of slowing so I quickly sidestepped out of the way to allow him free passage. However he did slow then stop probably about another twenty metres past me. I looked at the bike which looked an expensive racing variety.

'I'm sorry to stop you. I'm lost. I'm looking for Rosebery Terrace. Do you know where it is?'

The rider dismounted, turned, wheeled the bike towards me and took off his helmet. Copious blonde hair cascaded out. He was a girl!

'Sorry, Rosebery where?'

'Thanks for stopping. Rosebery Terrace. It's a long road that backs onto the river. Once I get to the river I'll get my bearings OK.' Things were about to get worse.

'River? There's no river round here. What river?'

'The Brisbane River. My friends' house is on the river. It's at the bottom of their garden.'

'You've got me there. Tell you what though, I'll phone my husband. He'll know.'

In fact he didn't know either. He did however look at a map he had in the house and was able to give me directions once his wife had told him exactly where we were.

'So you're about 3km from where you want to be and about 2km from where you are. (Work that one out). This river, the Brisbane River did you say? It's about twenty minutes that way. Can't say I've ever noticed it. Oh well gotta go. Good luck.'

And she was off! Whoosh. I eventually found the river, Rosebery Terrace and the right house. Darkness was not far off and one of the boys was watering flowers with a hosepipe when I walked up the drive. Sushma soon appeared.

'Where have you been?!'

'I walked from the station. Let's just say I took the sightseeing route. Come here, give me a hug.'

I'm not sure what the moral of the tale is. Take your own map next time or what? It did however reinforce two things that I had already learnt about Australia and its inhabitants. Australia is bigger than you think. Everywhere is a journey, and I do mean everywhere. Secondly the bulk of its population lead very parochial and suburban lives, living and socialising for the most part within a small area. Unlike suburban England there are no Red Lions, White Harts and Crown Taverns. They simply do not exist. The folks next door and over the road are your mates and best friends. Not for nothing is Australia's most successful export called '*Neighbours.*'

FRIED PIGEON

Those Poms who persist in doing the football pools in the English summer when the familiar 'Arsenal versus Manchester United' is replaced by 'Juventus versus Barramundi Creek' will be only too aware of the alacrity with which Australian town planners have happily mixed and replaced older colonial names with indigenous and newer immigrant place names. Presumably this is a national effort to appease the liberal elite and the later arrivals from parts of Europe other than the British Isles. Examples are numerous, and many roll off the tongue quite happily, like Canberra of the former and Sorrento of the latter, which neatly explains how you can end up with Juventus playing Barramundi Creek in a soccer match. Indeed so familiar have many indigenous names become, such as Canberra and Wooloomooloo, that they no longer appear to sound anything other than everyday places, like say Manly or Carlton.

Indeed, many of the older colonial names have often disappeared altogether, and one such name is Rose Hill, which being founded in 1788, was the second-oldest penal colony in Australia, and only months younger than Sydney. Its new name is Parramatta and I'm willing to bet a few cold ones that millions of young Australians don't even know that it had a former name. Having read '*Vinegar Hill*', the excellent novel by Colin Free, long before I ever set foot in Australia, I was thus determined to visit Rose Hill, now Parramatta, when the opportunity arose.

I had two choices, to go by train on the commuter line or take the boat from Circular Quay. Now I like 'trains and boats and planes', as Billy J. Kramer once sang, but as a sailor's son I really had no option. Besides, a glance at the aquatic route map told me that the boat to Parramatta would take me past Cockatoo Island, which I wanted to see, if only from a distance.

I walked from the hotel to the Darling Harbour stop and got on the next ferry that came along. It was not direct, but via Luna Park on the North Shore where it stopped before cutting back under the famous Sydney Harbour Bridge, Gazing upwards through the girders were human flies actually paying good money to 'walk over the hump', dressed in orange jump suits like suspected terrorists. Rather them than me I thought at the time.

On reaching Circular Quay, I was slightly annoyed to find that I had almost an hour's wait for the connection to Parramatta. I got a cold drink and an ice-cream and watched the waterborne world go by. I took a close look at some of the green and white harbour ferries as they scuttled to and fro, seemingly in every direction. I was intrigued to see one called *Scarborough*, which is where I come from in Yorkshire. An eighty-something old chap sitting on the bench seat near me looked as if he'd been in Sydney since before the War, but which War I wasn't sure.

'Excuse me, who got to name the harbour ferries, do you know?' He looked vacant, so I spoke up a bit. Perhaps he was a bit Mutton Jeff.

'These ferries, are they named after people or namesakes of other places? I'm from Scarborough myself, in England.' He livened up.

'Oh right, mate. No, not places, mate. Ships. They're all named after the First Fleet. All of 'em. Gotta go, mate, my boat's here.'

Where he was going to I've no idea, but it obviously wasn't Parramatta. I'd heard a lot about the 'First Fleet.' What visitor to Australia hasn't? The fleet of eleven vessels that took over two hundred and fifty days to sail from England to Botany Bay conveyed around fourteen hundred souls. Direct descendants of those earliest settlers call themselves 'First Fleeters', and even in 'Egalitarian Australia' regard themselves as a cut above later immigrants, even though many will have been descended from convicts. That's Australia for you!

My boat to Parramatta eventually arrived and departed Circular Quay with the regulatory three blasts on the whistle to announce she was going into reverse. It was all very efficient and nostalgic, reminiscent to me at least, of Hong Kong's Star Ferry, on which I had travelled a thousand times as a schoolboy. Even the ferries are the same colour – green and white. A half an hour later, and after a stop en route we sailed past Cockatoo Island to our left. I had wanted to see it as my Dad had mentioned on numerous occasions that his own ship, the destroyer HMS *Quilliam,* had paid off there in 1945.

In wartime it was a hive of activity, no doubt, and indeed for many years thereafter, the famous Aussie destroyer *Vampire* actually having been built there. I wished my Dad was still with us so I could tell him I had seen Cockatoo Island but sadly he had 'crossed the bar' only a few years earlier. I'm sure he was with me in spirit, though, along with his 'oppo' Leading Telegraphist Reg Clarkson.

With *Quilliam* paid off, they both had to wait several months for a civvy ship to take them back to Blighty, and like hundreds of other sailors were hosted by Australian families all over New South Wales. Their hosts were a Dr. Mason and his family in Tumut NSW, and to this day I have a super photo of Victor (my Dad) & Reg, both in uniform, taken in Tumut in 1945. Any descendants of Dr Mason are welcome to a copy, as is Tumut Town Hall, because it is also part of the town's history.

My little ferry carried about fifty passengers and had only a very shallow draught, probably little more than a metre. A sign at Circular Quay had given due warning that at certain times of the year when water in the creek was low and depending on tidal conditions, then there might be insufficient depth of water and accordingly part of the return journey might have to be by bus!

We headed west and inland as the river, or creek more like it, became narrower and shallower. Bird spotters will have noticed egrets and cormorants on the banks, eager to take advantage of unsuspecting fish in the shallow waters. Tall, shiny office buildings came into view and this was obviously 'downtown Parramatta', which was not what I was expecting from the site of the second oldest penal colony in New South Wales.

An hour after leaving Sydney, the boat pulled into a basin that was obviously the end of the line, so to speak, and we all got off. A hand-chalked sign announced that there would be no more return trips due to the tidal situation, and it gave the times of replacement buses. I made a mental note of the times and allowed myself two hours for a good look around. It didn't occur to me to find out where these buses actually departed from, which caused a bit of a problem later.

I found a 'visitor's map' on a large notice board and studied it hard for a few minutes. Being a decent geographer, I have always found maps easy to read and remember, but this one completely floored me. The large arrow that said 'YOU ARE HERE' was fine, but the river was exactly where it definitely wasn't. I was flummoxed. Then after a while it dawned on me that whereas ninety-nine percent of maps have a compass rose that points north, for some crazy reason this one pointed south. Once I had reoriented my own personal compass accordingly, I set out north (or was it south?) up a Charles Street and then turned into a Church Street. Sure enough there was a church at the very end on a corner. So far so good.

It was hot, and I was thirsty and hungry, my budget hotel's lack of breakfast taking its toll on my well-being. Deciding to kill two birds with one stone to stave off thirst and starvation, I walked into an Italian café called Liana's. The female assistant was friendly enough, and obviously second or third generation Italian-Australian.

'Yeah, there's only outside tables now. It's quite busy. There's one take that.'

Fortunately it had an umbrella to provide shade, as the time was by now about oneish and the sun at its meridian. In Anglo-Saxon that means it was so fekking hot you could fry eggs on a car roof. A waitress came and I ordered two beers, such was my thirst. She returned with two beers and two glasses. Did she think I was going to offer one to a passer-by? I gave the menu a cursory glance and then ordered my default dish – spaghetti bolognese. You can't go wrong with a 'spag bol', and it was available in small, medium and large portions. I was hungry, gluttony was in the air, and I opted for the last one.

'Are you sure? They are very large.'

I took her word for it and pointed to a bloke at an adjacent table, who I could see was a fellow 'spag bol' fan.'

'That's a medium.' It looked big enough to me, so I came down a notch.

'And another beer please, if I may.' The first one hadn't touched the sides.

'Are you sure? It's very hot today.'

Was this girl a volunteer in the NSW Health Police? Surely the hotter the day, the more beer you needed. In any case, for the most part I found Australian beers were served in ludicrously small amounts, a schooner being about the size of a sherry glass my Granny used to drink Crofts Original from. Oh well, when in Rome, or even Parramatta.

I didn't have to wait long for either the beer or the 'spag bol', and the latter sure was worth waiting for. It was simply divine, and proved two things for me – that you don't have to be in Europe to sample excellent Italian food, and that not all Italian immigrants went to Melbourne!

Digressing, I must tell you this little side-story. A couple of years ago I was in a Lucia's Café in York, England. All the staff bar one were Italians, the sole exception being an Aussie girl in her early twenties called Mel. That's what it said on her name-tag. She came to serve my friend and me and I said something like:

'Thanks, Melanie, I'll start with the....'

'My name's not Melanie eckshully....the girls call me that cos I'm from Mairlben.'

'Oh, right. Sorry. What a jolly good job you're not from Wagga Wagga.'

It took a little while to sink in before she gave a slight grin. I wasn't convinced she fully 'got it', but maybe she originally came from Tasmania.

Anyway, back to Parramatta. I went into the café to pay the bill and 'Liana' asked me if I had enjoyed it. I told her, without any exaggeration, that it was the best 'spag bol' I had ever tasted anywhere.

'Do you have any secret ingredients, you know, your own recipe?'

'No, we don't. It might just be the very high quality of our beef. It's locally produced.'

It was only much later that I learned that the decamping of the early settlers from Sydney Cove to Rose Hill was advised due to the massive contrast in fertility of the soil in the area surrounding the latter. That made sense. Good soil equals good grass equals good beef equals good 'spag bol.' I was impressed to such an extent that I mentioned Liana's in my novel *Her Place in the Sun,* which I wrote immediately following my return to Blighty.

I walked back down Church Street – don't ask me if it was north or south – and paused to look in a small jeweller's window for a pressie for a friend. However, like almost all of Australia on a Saturday afternoon it was shut. Finding my way back to the normal point of departure for the boat, I studied again the replacement bus timetable. I had just missed one. Bugger! I took solace with a coffee and a glass of iced water in a small café which also had a good selection of paperback books. Who knows, maybe one day my book of short stories, including this one, will end up in that shop. That sure would be nice.

A half an hour later I found the bus stop in Charles Street and travelled a few kilometres to the next stop down river which did have sufficient depth of water to take us back to Central Sydney. This time Cockatoo Island was on our right, and as I passed it, I raised an imaginary tot of rum to my Dad and Reg.

Stepping off the boat onto terra firma once again, I spotted the octogenarian I had chatted to much earlier in the day. He recognised me, and we exchanged greetings. I told him that I had found Parramatta an interesting place and that I would like to return one day. There were dozens of pigeons flying around and zooming in on any crumbs or fragments of ice cream cone dropped onto the floor. Amazingly, several of them seemed to have 'club feet' and quite how they managed to balance while walking was remarkable.

'Do you think they've been in scraps with dogs or cats?' I enquired.

'No mate, it's quite common round here. The stupid bastards have settled on live electricity wires which have fried their feet.'

'Fried pigeon! Sounds tasty.'

'Yeah. I like 'em in a pie, myself.'

To this day I'm not sure if he was joking or not.

THE SHOT TOWER

I was in Tasmania, of all places. Somebody has to go there. Actually, I'm being unfair. Although the butt of many a joke, the 'Island State' is an Aussie national treasure. An absolute diamond. Lying some two hundred miles south of Melbourne, where they play tennis, watch Neighbours and consume cappuccinos by the litre, Tasmania is a land of dreams and myth. It is to Australia what the Isle of Wight is to England – part of it but quite separate from it in terms of geography, latitude and attitude.

I flew to Hobart from Tullamarine Airport, Melbourne, on the breakfast flight. It is the only time I've been served cornflakes at thirty thousand feet. Just before landing the Captain reminded us that although the time in Tasmania was the same, we should wind our clocks back at least thirty years. I had spent only a short time on the ground before I knew what he meant.

The airport terminal reminded me of Stornoway, Isle of Lewis, except that it was sunny and warm and the damp Celtic mists blowing off the Minch were thankfully absent. My hosts, Derek and Pam, were there to meet me and were determined to show me what they could of Hobart in the all-too- short duration of my stay. A trip to Mount Wellington in the afternoon was followed by a fabulous seafood dinner at the famous *Drunken Admiral* that evening. The harbour and Derwent River were wonderful. It was just after a nightcap before we turned in for the night when Derek said

'I think I'll take you to the Shot Tower tomorrow, Mark. OK?'

What could I say? I didn't even know what a shot tower was.

'Pam isn't too steady on her pins, Mark' said Derek after breakfast the next morning. 'It's just you and me on this one, mate.'

My suspicions were more than a little aroused. It was a sunny day again, and we merrily followed the winding coastal route south from home towards an area called Sandy Bay. We finally pulled up at what looked like a stone lighthouse. I thought this was more than a little odd. I have seen lighthouses located slightly inland to avoid coastal erosion, but this one was at least half a mile from the sea and unlike its thousands of cousins worldwide was stone grey in colour and not painted in high visibility white. There was a small car park with only two other cars in sight.

'This is it,' chirped Derek. 'Have you been to a shot tower before?'

I decided to come clean.

'You'll have to tell me, Derek. Just what is a shot tower?'

My imagination was running wild by now. Tasmanian prisons were reputed to be the toughest in the whole of Australia in the early settlement days, but if they wanted to shoot a prisoner, then why not perform the ghastly deed at ground level? Why did they have to drag the poor sod up a wannabe lighthouse first before shooting him? The Tower of London wasn't all that high, and they dispatched plenty of felons there almost at sea level.

'You don't know? You're joking! It's where they made shot. You know...musket balls.'

I was still failing to make the connection. History had never been my strongest subject, but plainly my education was lacking something somewhere. It wasn't long before the gap in my knowledge was filled.

'It's seven dollars per person, dear. No concessions for seniors', announced the lady behind the reception desk, who didn't even look up as she continued reading a book.

I rummaged in my pockets and retrieved a ten dollar bill and four one dollar coins. She gave us each a little pink ticket that reminded me of a sixties-style cinema ticket before an usherette with a torch ripped it in half and shoved you into the smoke-filled gloom.

'Go through that door there.'

She pointed towards a wooden door that would not have looked out of place on a garden shed that hadn't been creosoted for fifty years. The latch had a metal thumb press that had been worn down smooth by a hundred-thousand thumbs. The combination of old wood and old metal gave the whole shebang the air of the gallows. It was creepy.

'Oh yeah' the lady bellowed just as we entered the dimness beyond the door. 'I almost forgot to say. There's a prize if you count correctly exactly how many steps there are to the top.'

In front of us in the perpetual twilight, stretched a spiral staircase. As it corkscrewed to the left it ascended, and to the right it descended. The handrail looked old but sturdy enough. I peered over it and about fifty feet below it in a dimly-lit sort of cellar I was able to make out what looked a bit like an old iron bath except that it was round and about six feet across. Derek finally enlightened me.

'So how they made lead musket balls was like this. You melt ingots of lead up at the top and then pour the molten metal into a colander which is suspended over the drop right at the top. The liquid metal then falls through the holes forming almost perfect spheres as it does so. These then rapidly cool as they fall the several hundred feet down the tower into the tub of water below where they are then collected as shot. The bigger the holes in the colander, the bigger the calibre of shot. Got it?'

It seemed almost too easy, but the enterprising Scottish engineer who had built the Tower with prison labour in the mid 19th century obviously had a canny eye for profit. Supplying the Military and the Admiralty with shot from what was at the time the highest shot tower in the southern hemisphere must have have made him a rich man.

Armed with this new found knowledge, I was now determined to follow in the footsteps of a thousand convicts and climb to the top.

You go first, Derek.'

'OK, Mark but we'll both keep count separately and see if we get the same answer. Agreed?'

'Yep. Off you go then.'

Although in his seventies, Derek was quite nimble and started climbing up at a fair pace. We both soon realised that the Greek bloke "Pi" and his formulae for radii, circumferences and the like meant that if you walked on the inside of the spiral you had a lot less ground to cover than if you walked on the outside. However, it did have its psychological downside, as every now and again you were tempted to look up the tower where there seemed to be a suggestion of natural light at the top. The light never seemed to get any nearer. It was as dim as a glow worm's armpit.

Silently but methodically we both kept count. A hundred and nine, a hundred and ten, a hundred and eleven...With every step there was a loud creak as the one hundred and fifty year old Tasmanian oak steps took the strain of my excessive hundred kilos. It was most unnerving.

'Excuse me, sorry!'

An alien female voice came out of the dimness. Somebody else was coming down! We both moved out to the wall side to allow her to pass as she clung to the inner railing. To our surprise the stone was freezing. How could it be? It was thirty degrees Celsius outside even at ten in the morning. The lady, probably aged about forty, brushed past us and continued downwards into the gloom. We hadn't even seen her face. We both paused for breath.

'Let's have a conference shall we?' suggested Derek. 'How many do you make it so far?'

'A hundred and eleven. You?'

'Bugger, no. A hundred and twelve!'

'Yes, but you're a step higher than me.'

'I know, but I took that into consideration when I stepped aside to let the lady pass. Did you?'

I wasn't sure. If anything I thought I might have gone down a step not up as I moved across to the outer handrail affixed to the stone.

'Let's stick with where we both think we are and review at the top.'

A hundred and ninety nine. Two hundred! We both stopped at a narrow gap in the stonework which afforded a slit-eyed view of the Derwent River estuary. We gasped through the slit for a few lungfuls of fresh air. It was almost cold. How high were we? My ears had popped by now. Five minutes later and we were both at the top.

'Two hundred and fifty eight. You?'

'Two hundred and sixty. Blimey!'

'Look, we've got another chance to double-check' said Derek. 'We'll count again on the way down.'

The platform at the top afforded three hundred and sixty degrees of panoramic views, but it was freezing, and we both shivered in our short-sleeved shirts. We took in the vista for a couple of minutes and then began the descent, taking care to keep proper count. One, two, three...

We both knew something was wrong when we both reached three hundred. Unbelievably, we had sailed past the wooden door we came through in the first instance and were heading rapidly for the cellar and the bathtub. By now totally innumerate and disorientated, we decided nonetheless to take a waterless bath. At the bottom we peered skyward. It was like looking through a telescope the wrong way. We cut our losses and climbed back up to the wooden door and into the reception area. We both noticed that the previously-illuminated neon red 'EXIT' sign on the back of the door had gone out. We complained to the lady, who seemed to have finished reading.

'Yeah, it does go out from time to time, that red light. Don't tell me you ended up at the bottom! Anyway, never mind. Let's see if you won the prize. How many steps were there to the top?'

We decided to take an average.

'Two hundred and fifty nine.'

'Sorry chaps. The right answer is two hundred and fifty eight.'

'Bugger! What was the prize anyway, just out of interest?'

'A free ticket to walk back up again.'

She picked up her book and started reading again. And they say Tasmanians don't have a sense of humour!

IS SHE WORTH IT?

Decades ago, as a small boy, I regularly visited my Uncle Allan Danby, who spent many lonely hours doing jigsaws. A former Yorkshire farmer he was deprived of a normal retirement by a drunk driver and as a result spent many years in a sedentary state. Crosswords and jigsaws were a major part of his entertainment, and it was he who first introduced me to 'Jigraphy', the combined world of jigsaws and maps. On one particular afternoon I found him doing a 1,000 piece map of Australia. He always welcomed visitors, and greeted me with:

'Now then, lad, you'll have to help me with this one. It's harder than t'others by a long road.'

I studied the box lid, as you do, to get the overall picture, and Uncle Allan had already completed the outer frame of the jigsaw, which, being composed entirely of 'straight-edged pieces', was the easy bit.

I can still picture the whole thing. It was very colourful, I recall, and copiously illustrated with images around all four borders on all four sides to depict stereotypes of people and places that the average person would easily relate to. Off the coast of north Western Australia was a pearl diver, probably in the vicinity of Broome. Off south Western Australia was a whaling ship, probably somewhere near Albany. Aboriginals were everywhere inland and shown throwing boomerangs at kangaroos and everything that moved. The Sydney Harbour Bridge was also prominent, as were several lifeguards at Bondi Beach. You get the general drift, I'm sure.

But the image that stuck the most in my mind was the caricature of opal miners in a small South Australian township called Coober Pedy. Men with bush hats, pickaxes, shovels and Tilley lamps, clawing their way through sandstone, left an image with me that I have retained to this day. So how on earth does that lead to this little story?

It's funny how the human brain automatically associates certain metals and minerals with certain countries. Think diamonds, think South Africa. Think emeralds, think Columbia. Think opals, think Australia! Apart from Coober Pedy, I'd heard about a place called Quilpie in Queensland. It was also renowned for the quality of its opals – that I did know. Boulder opals, to be geologically precise.

So, on spotting a shop called Quilpie Opals whilst wandering the streets of Brisbane's CBD, I decided the opportunity to pop in was too good to miss. It was mid-afternoon, hot and very quiet. I entered the shop, which seemed eerily quiet. I walked slowly around the biggish sales area and gazed at some of the most beautiful stones I had ever seen. I was transfixed, and my mind flashed back to that jigsaw and my by now late Uncle Allan. A middle-aged chap appeared, obviously the proprietor.

'G'day, can I help you?'

'I'd just like a look around, please, if I may. I feel like a kid in a sweetshop. They are so beautiful.'

'No worries, by all means. Just shout if you want to know anything, mate.'

Probably for a quarter of an hour, maybe longer, I meandered around the whole shop. I decided to buy my two goddaughters back in England, Millie and Lucy, a small pendant each. I knew I had missed Lucy's birthday anyway whilst I was in Australia, so this would make amends.

'Excuse me, can I take a closer look at these here, please?' The chap walked over and smiled.

'I've never known anyone look so closely. Do you know a lot about opals? I'm Paul, by the way. Paul Burton.' We shook hands.

'England, I take it? On holiday?'

'Yes, on both counts. Visiting a few friends here and taking a good look around. You born and bred in Brissie?'

'The family originally came from the English Midlands, but I was born here in Queensland.'

'Maybe your mob came from Burton on Trent, hence your surname.'

'Dunno mate. Could be.'

'Burton on Trent is the centre of the English brewing industry', I threw in for a laugh. He grinned.

'Is that right? Well, my grandfather was one of the original opal prospectors in south west Queensland in the early nineteen hundreds. Would you like to see some photographs?'

You bet I would. Paul walked over to a wall-mounted cabinet and opened the doors wide to reveal the most amazing black and white photographs. It was bush hats, pickaxes and Tilley lamps all over again, almost half a century after doing the jigsaw. I felt very privileged to be shown them. These were family artefacts of the highest order. Paul's forbears would be very proud of the care he was taking of them and the pride he demonstrated when showing them to others, like me, who had never been closer to an opal mine than a mere jigsaw. I told him about Millie and Lucy and he helped me choose two nice moderately-priced pendants. He wrapped them for me and I settled the bill.

'Now, Mark, would you like to see the best ones we have?'

He removed some from a secure drawer and laid them on a cloth on a counter top. I gave out a long, low whistle. Oh wow! There was one in particular, about two centimetres square, that glowed like an emerald. To the layman, it could even have been one. I had to ask.

'Is this one for sale? If so how much?'

'To be fair, I wouldn't take less than four thousand dollars for it. You look like a generous bloke. Why don't you buy it for the wife back home?' He was pulling my leg.

'Actually I'm not married!'

'Well in that case your girlfriend, then...she'll be over the moon with that one.' I mulled over what he'd said and decided on a humorous response.

'Nah, she's probably not worth *that* much, mate!'

Suddenly a new voice, a female one, arrived out of the ether.

'I heard that, and I'm sure she is, Mark!'

Behind the counter and sitting in what must have been a very low chair was a lovely-looking lady, very smart and well-spoken with perfect olive skin. She stood up, reached across the counter and gently shook hands.

'I'm Melita, Paul's wife.'

I was taken aback, to say the least.

'You must be Maltese, with the name Melita?'

'Really, why's that?'

'Melita is the old Roman name for Malta. It means the Island of Honey. Didn't you know that?'

'Actually, no, I didn't. My family is originally from Sicily.'

I told her that Malta was my birthplace, and we chatted animatedly for several minutes. Then Paul brought me some more pictures and artefacts to look at. I cannot tell you how long I spent in the shop. It was just surreal. I bade them farewell and promised to visit again, with Melita's final words still ringing in my ears to this day:

'When you find a girl who is worth that opal, come back, won't you?'

I just might, too.

AUSTRALIA AND MALTA

As a small boy living on the island of Malta, where my father worked for the Admiralty, I had been amazed, even puzzled, by the seemingly endless connections with Australia. What on earth did a two hundred square mile island have to do with a three million square mile continent ten thousand miles away?

The paper shop in St Paul's Bay was called 'Kangaroo Newsagents,' the theatre at St. Andrew's barracks was called Australia Hall, the air was thick with *Canberra* bombers from RAF Luqa, and even the P & O liner *Canberra* had put into Grand Harbour on her maiden voyage to Australia, albeit because a major fire on board had necessitated emergency repairs. Our flat landlords, Charles and Walter Bezzina, had earned their money to invest in property by working on the Queensland sugar plantations. And therein lies part of the mystery. People.

Catholic Malta, just like Catholic Ireland, produced lots and lots of sons and daughters, and thus people became one of her biggest exports. Whereas the Irish looked west to America, so the Maltese looked east to Australia. With Malta being en route from England to the Lucky Country, there was no shortage of vessels to carry the thousands of adventurers who sailed to the promised land. Some came back, like the Bezzinas, but thousands stayed and in so doing took their culture, and more importantly their genetic bloodlines, with them.

No European peoples have a more interesting and varied DNA than the Maltese. Having being invaded by the Greeks, Phoenicians, Arabs, Carthaginians, French and finally the British, the Maltese gene pool is a treasure trove of human antiquity. And that is why Australia today contains within its population hundreds of thousands of people of the most historic bloodlines. Sadly, most of them don't know that, let alone appreciate it.

In my book 'Malta: My Island' I mentioned meeting a real estate salesman in Perth called Paul Azzopardi. He was as Aussie as you can get, a very pleasant young man and probably third generation. But he didn't have a clue about Malta. His forbears might as well have come from the Moon. I came across many Maltese names in WA – Galea, Sciberas, Falzon to name but a few. But when I flew cross-country to Brisbane, Queensland, even I was in for a surprise.

I think I was on my second day in the State capital and enjoying every moment. Taking a long walk by the magnificent river, I paused with a cold drink for a rest in the heat on a bench. Always keen to strike up a conversation with the locals, I started chatting to a bloke, probably around sixty years old. I don't know what a resident is supposed to look like, as opposed to a tourist, but he looked like he lived there. I was right.

He was right about me, too. I was indeed a Pom on holiday – the sunburnt neck and nose probably giving me away at a hundred metres. Ends up he was a newly-retired Qantas pilot. The conversation was easy both ways. As a Jumbo pilot he had seen much of the world, mostly from a bird's viewpoint, so to speak, but he was of course familiar with many of the world's countries and cities. Now, one of the most eye-catching buildings on the banks of the Brisbane River is the State Parliament Building. You simply can't miss it. Like the Sydney Harbour Bridge, which flies the State Flag of New South Wales atop its highest point, so the building in question flies the State Flag of Queensland.

Like all Australian flags it was visually stunning, particularly in the sunshine. And slap bang in the middle of the flag is a bloody great Maltese Cross. This had taken me totally by surprise. Why? I asked my newly made pilot friend if he knew why.

'I have no idea mate, to be honest. Must be a historical thing. Tell you what though, you could always pop into the Parliament Building and ask them. Why don't you?'

So I did just that, the next day, in fact. And do you know what? Nobody had a bloody clue. They just took it as read, as it were. It was quite shocking. The Maltese Cross is in fact an ancient heraldic emblem and associated with the Cathars, Hospitallers, Knights of St. John and latterly by the State of Malta which has 'adopted' it as its own.

Enquiries and a bit of online research revealed that the Queensland State Flag originally portrayed a head of Queen Victoria. She had already had a State in her name, so the newer State was simply called 'Queen's Land' as a second-best solution – to keep her amused, presumably.

However, human heads, whether of the royal or commoner variety, are not the easiest of things to draw, so when Queen Vic died in 1901 the decision was taken (by who I do not know) to replace the royal head with the Maltese Cross. I haven't found the answer as to why the Cross was chosen. It is not the easiest of things to draw, being a sixteen-sided depiction of four arrow heads pointing to a centre. I am still uncertain, but the answer may have a naval or maritime background. Did some of Malta's earliest migrants take the Cross with them to remind them of home so far away? In my book I asked for 'answers on a postcard', but to date none have showed up.

Mind you, that's hardly surprising, given the state of Australia Post. For the next few days, in fact the duration of my stay in the lovely city of Brisbane, I asked everyone from bartenders to museum curators if they knew the origin of the Cross on their State Flag. Not a single person could offer the merest hint of an answer. That is a pretty damning indictment of ignorance. Or perhaps, and more likely, it is a simple reflection of Queenslanders in general, who are for the most part totally relaxed, laid back in the extreme, and generally don't give a Four XXXX about what happens to them, let alone the rest of the world.

On my last day in Brisbane I took a taxi to the airport, located well east of the CBD and at least a twenty-minute drive. I had a brainwave. I'll ask the driver. Taxi drivers know everything, don't they? The driver, Mike, was a family man in his late fifties and had lived all his life in Brisbane and its environs. There was almost nothing he didn't know about Brissie and its people. I waited until we were almost at Eagle Farm before posing the sixty-four thousand dollar question. Why was the Maltese Cross on the State Flag of Queensland? His eyes and face screwed up for what seemed an eternity. At long last was I about to discover the answer? Fingers crossed.

'To be honest, mate, I hadn't even bloody noticed.'

You see what I mean about Queenslanders?

THE BAT

I had five whole days to spend in Sydney, or 'Sinny.' as the locals call it. Having received lots of conflicting advice about where to go and what to see, I wasn't too sure what to do. In the end I just followed my nose, which is what I do best.

Naval affairs having always been close to my heart I decided that a 'must see' was the Australian Maritime Museum in Darling Harbour. I was fortunate that my budget hotel (so budget that brekky wasn't even on the menu) was within ten minutes walk of the museum. So after a coffee and a bread roll from a café a short walk away which, I ate sat on a pavement bench, I set off down Lime Street through a gap next to the Head Office of the Macquarie Bank and found myself looking onto the harbour.

It was only tennish in the morning and a lovely sunny day. It was hot but not 'Perth hot', and I didn't find myself grabbing for a water bottle every few minutes. I had just flown down from Brisbane with its noted high humidity, and Sydney's climate seemed a tad more agreeable to a Sunburnt Pom like myself.

Turning left at the waterfront I followed a long and wide boardwalk that must be trying to compete with its Atlantic City counterpart for reputation. I was amazed at the number of expensive-looking vessels berthed alongside, with hardly enough room between them for a cigarette paper, let alone the ubiquitous crush-proof black rubber tyres. Most of the boats seemed to be geared up for entertaining, with capacious glass staterooms for evening soirées, cocktail parties and the like.

Everything seemed to be tourist industry slanted. There were no fishing boats, work-boats or anything that even faintly resembled normal commerce and industry. It was different on the other side of the harbour a mere hundred metres or so away. All the berthed vessels looked, well let's say somewhat dated. Suddenly it dawned on me. That must be the museum!

One of the ships was much bigger than the others – a very impressive warship whose silhouette looked almost familiar to me. It occurred to me that it was the former HMAS *Vendetta*, a destroyer that had served in the Royal Australian Navy in the sixties and seventies and which I had seen many times in the naval basin in Hong Kong. Things were looking up, as in addition to going on board the life-sized replica of the Bark *Endeavour,* I would be able to renew my acquaintance with the *Vendetta.*

Several years earlier I had been in Whitby, North Yorkshire, with my father, when *Endeavour* was paying a historic visit to the port which was the original vessel's point of departure for her Master, Captain James T. Cook, before he started his exploratory voyages to Australia and the Pacific. Sadly the queues to go on board her made those for rationed bread in the London blitz look minor by comparison, and we had decided not to bother. Dad had since 'crossed the bar', but I was determined to visit *Endeavour* on behalf of both of us.

I kept walking along the boardwalk and passed the renowned Sydney Aquarium on my left. Restaurants and eateries were numerous but were mostly Chinese, Thai or whatever. I didn't see any Aussie steak joints. In fact I hardly saw any Aussies at all. Nearly everyone seemed to be Chinese or Japanese. It dawned on me then when I had left Brisbane and the girl on the hotel reception had said 'enjoy China.' They were just everywhere. Now I don't speak any Mandarin, but having lived in Hong Kong for years I know the difference between spoken Cantonese and Mandarin when I hear it. These people were all talking as if they were gargling with a glass full of wasps, so definitely Mandarin. They were not post-handover Hong Kongers seeking a new life. Were they all tourists? Or maybe they had already bought most of New South Wales with the proceeds from zillions of cellphones and computers. I have to say I found it a trifle disconcerting even though I was just a Pommy tourist in a former colony. Oh well, no worries, as the locals would undoubtedly say.

I arrived at a very long and ornate bridge – the Pyrmont Bridge – which allows pedestrians the opportunity to cut across Cockles Bay to the 'west bank', as it were, thus saving a walk of perhaps an extra kilometre or more. To my surprise I spotted a modern if small warship, to me obviously a mine-hunter, on the inside of the Bay. How the heck did it get there when the arches forming the Bridge's structure were much lower than the vessel's masts, I asked myself?

I started walking across the Bridge, and at about the half-way point I drew level with this modern-looking example of the Royal Australian Navy's ships. The pennant number painted in white near her bow with a black shadow was 82, that I do remember and I was minded to look up her actual name in my Jane's Fighting Ships when I got home to the UK. In the event I didn't have to because I soon spotted a shiny nameplate revealing her name as *Huon*, named after a river in Tasmania. Being a wine buff, as well as a ship spotter I knew the Huon River was famed for its Rieslings.

About half a dozen of the crew, male and female, were on the weather deck in tropical 'whites' uniform and seemed quite relaxed. They were clearly very laid-back about being stuck behind the Bridge. I certainly couldn't see any other exit to the main harbour beyond. I thought I would try a bit of friendly banter, so I waved and attracted the attention of one of the female officer's.

'Hello, *Huon,* you're a long way from home aren't you? Tassie's that way!' I pointed south behind them. One of the girls shouted back.

'Yeah, you're right there, mate, but we're here for a few more days yet. It's an official port visit.'

I pointed to the Bridge and, keeping as straight a face as I could, shouted:

'How the heck are you going to get out? In fact, how the heck did you get in?'

This seemed to cause immediate merriment amongst them and one of the males shouted back.

'It's a swing bridge, mate. How the xxxx do you think we got in?'

I felt a complete eejit, waved again and walked on. This Antipodean sun must be getting to me. Ten minutes later I arrived at the Museum proper and made my way to the cashier's booth.

'Right, what kind of ticket do you want to buy, mate?'

Would he have said 'mate' to a Chinese visitor? Who knows? I was uncertain what he meant.

'Er well, just for the day please. I don't want a season ticket.' The man behind the desk didn't smile.

'I mean do you want to see the exhibits on dry land or do you want to go on board some of the vessels? That's extra.'

I was beginning to get his drift.

'Well I sure do want to go on-board the *Endeavour,* as when I was in Whitby...'

'OK, mate, we're getting there slowly.'

It was just as well I wasn't speaking Mandarin. I wondered how a visiting Chink would cope with this Strine speaker.'

'Jew wanna go on the *Bat*? That's more extra, mate.'

Did he mean the boat? If so, which boat?

'Yes, I would like to go on the boat please.'

'Listen, mate, if you do want to go on the former HMAS *Vampire,* then there's a small extra charge. Now do you or don't you?'

Slowly but surely, the penny dropped. I had mistaken the *Vampire, "the Bat,"* for her sister ship the *Vendetta.* Two howlers in such a short period of time. First the Bridge and now the Bat. It just wasn't my day.

I bought a commemorative wooden plaque of HMAS *Vampire*'s ship's crest depicting a silver bat with her motto 'Audamus' inscribed beneath. It adorns my office wall as a reminder of a memorable experience. I often wonder what the Mandarin is for Bat.

SIMMOS

'You just *have* to go to Mandurah, Mark. It's the in place to go. I've got a busy day tomorrow, so why don't you go on your own? You can take the Suzuki jeep if you like.'

No way! Lynne's jeep was like many a radioactive isotope and had a half-life of about half a day. I'll take the train. I like trains. So once again I took the bus to Stirling Station and the train to Murray Street in the CBD where I changed trains for one going all the way to Mandurah, a new resort about forty kilometres south of Perth. It was a very hot day indeed and felt just as hot as the 'meltdown walk' in Fremantle a couple of days earlier. Surely it wasn't going to be as hot, was it? Not forty-two Celsius again?

The smart new train zipped south at a swift rate of knots and from memory made only a couple of stops. We went through a place called Applecross which I had remembered from one of Lynne's famous 'Club Walks.' I had made a mental note never to go on one of those again. Some male teacher who had assumed the role of Team Leader had taken it upon himself to be my chaperon and had bored the arse off me for the duration of the hour's walk to a huge pub called the Windsor Arms.

It had been an evening walk and afforded nice views of the sun setting over the Swan River. In other words the sun was most definitely over the yardarm. When we reached the pub I was staggered to see everyone reach into their bags for bottles of mineral water and those concrete-emulating mineral bars. You must be joking! I emerged from the bar with two proper pints of real Swan Lager. The first one didn't hit the sides and it was good not to be apologised to by bar staff with the words: 'I'm afraid we only sell boutique beers now.'

At last, a real pub. The teacher was appalled, and turned down flat my offer to buy him one. I hope he enjoyed his designer water at about four dollars a litre. When this clown tried to tell me that Perth, WA's capital, was a lot bigger than London I decided to ask him what subject he taught. I thought maybe something trendy like natural history or environmental studies. When he told me that he taught geography, I decided to give him a wide berth. Anyway, enough of that, back to Mandurah. Or at least the journey there.

Once we had put the Swan estuary and its creeks behind us we headed more or less south, and the land turned to the brownish scrub so prevalent and characteristic of Western Australia. Looking at it from the comfort of a modern air-conditioned train was a whole lot different to walking in it outside. It even looked hot, with that shimmering glow of air rising from just about everything.

We passed places called Bull Creek and Cockburn Central as we sped south. I was disappointed that the line wasn't closer to the coast, as I was hoping to glimpse the naval facilities at Garden Island and Henderson. I had recently read and digested a promotional brochure all about the latter, which had the rather grand and unusual title of the Common User Facility. I thought it was odd that its title didn't give any clue whatsoever about what this facility actually did. So for those of you who don't know, it is a joint civil, military and naval dockyard project which has the ability to 'lift' large vessels as big as destroyers and frigates clean out of the water and into the sanctuary of covered workshops which look rather like aircraft hangars.

To most tourists and visitors this would be at the bottom of their 'must see' list, but to me whose forbears built the *Titanic* and only two generations ago had fought at Jutland, Gallipoli and Zeebrugge and one generation earlier at Mirs el Kbir and Leyte Gulf, this was a major let-down. I would have dearly liked to visit both Henderson and Fleet Base West at Garden Island. Sadly, the only RAN contacts I'd ever had, had 'crossed the bar' a long time ago. Maybe one day.

It was good, though, to note that unlike the sea-blind goons that have governed the UK for decades, Australian politicians of whatever hue were investing heavily in the defence of their territorial waters and economic zones. Enough said. We passed through another development called Secret Harbour, which amused me as a sign post read just that. Some secret!

'Bing bong. This is Mandurah, this is Mandurah. This train termites here.'

So like everyone else I got off the train, expecting to be able to walk to the places of interest. Wrong, you had to take a bus which only ran about every half hour. I just followed the herd and boarded a bus that said BEACH on the front. I made a mental note of the number for the return journey. It wasn't far to go, maybe a couple of kilometres.

The bus stopped and we all had to get off. Those termites were at it again. Needless to say, I hadn't got a clue where I was or where I was going. I had a small, scruffy tourist guide map which was about as much use as a chocolate teapot.

There was no scale and no arrow pointing north. I'd been through all that lark in Hervey Bay, Queensland, and having no wish to repeat the experience I scrunched the so-called guide into my pocket. I walked down the side of a lake, or a lagoon as the map had referred to it. It was salt water, so must have had an outlet to the ocean somewhere.

'Schools of dolphins can frequently be spotted in the lagoon', according to the guide again. Yeah right. The water didn't look deep enough to me, but hey ho, you never know. I just wouldn't hold my breath, that's all. There were lots of new buildings on the far side of the lagoon, buildings which looked like very expensive apartment blocks to me. Were they owned and lived in by locals, I wondered? Or were they owned by property magnates who rented them out to Nips during chilly Honshu winters? You just never knew these days.

I came across a road called Dolphin Drive, so perhaps my dismissive musings earlier had been a tad premature. Everything seemed to be new and pristine, and unlike Freo, which was 'old', this place was brand spanking new, almost glaringly so.

Almost by accident I spotted the WA Sailing Museum, and a poster outside boasted that it contained the very yacht Australia II that had wrested the Americas Cup from the New York Yacht Club in Rhode Island USA in 1983. Sod the dolphins – now that did interest me. I searched for the way in, expecting and happy to have to pay a few bucks to look at a piece of yachting history. By coincidence I had actually been in Rhode Island in September 1983. When it started to look as if the Royal Perth Yacht Club might pull off the impossible and win, I was the butt of many a verbal attack from partisan Americans staring defeat in the face for the first time in a century.

'Hey you, asshole! Yes you. Are you from 'Oss Trailer?' We're gonna whip you, buddy. You'll wish you never reached the final.'

In the finest Queen's English I could muster, I would tell my assailant that I was a Limey. I was tempted to tell them that unlike Americans, Aussies do not live in Trailer Parks. They might live in Yew Nuts but definitely not Trailer Parks.

Unbelievably, I was told by an attendant that the museum was 'in reno' and closed all week. A jolly and large lady called Marie told me that she would personally show me round if I came back next week. Sadly, by then I would be back in the 'frozen north' of a Yorkshire winter, but her gesture was very much appreciated.

It was very hot, easily as hot as Freo had been. I was desperate for a cooling drink, and as the museum and its café were shut, I made my way back to where the bus had dropped us off and where I had noticed a café called Simmos. It had amused me, as I had a good friend back in Selby, Yorkshire, called David Simpson, who as often as not was called 'Simmo' by his mates. He would be delighted to know that a café in a plush Australian resort had been named after him.

Almost at boiling point, I went inside and bought, I kid you not, two beers, some cold water and a mango ice-cream. I walked out onto a decking area to sit under an umbrella. A middle-aged lady was pushing another lady in a wheelchair and she seemed to have caught the front wheels around the leg of a chair, a bit like a supermarket trolley with a brain of its own.

'Stay still, I'll move the table. Don't worry.'

I put the beers and water on a vacant table, clung onto the ice-cream with one hand, and yanked the anchoring table out of harm's way. My good deed for the day. I smiled and she smiled back.

'Thank you, young man.' Being in my fifties, that pleased me no end, but nothing prepared me for what she said next.

'Just a minute, I know you. You're from Scarborough. In Yorkshire. I stopped you to ask you the way to the cricket ground last year. July time. I'm right, aren't I?'

She was, too. Just how far do you have to go in this global village we now inhabit not to be recognised? She didn't buy me a beer, though. Mind you, I already had two to go at.

LES MURDIE

Sadly for me, the three-week trip Down Under, my first, was coming to an end. What a great time I'd had. On arrival the Immigration Officer, John, had said 'Come back and see us again.' Too right I would. It was early evening, 'my bags were packed and I was ready to go', as Peter, Paul & Mary had sung years earlier.

'Honk honk!'

The pre-ordered cab, appropriately a Swan Taxi, was outside. I said goodbye and thank you to Lynne, my host, and pecked her on the cheek. I declined the offer to do the same to her four cats, one of which, Kit Kat, had tried to eat my toast that morning.

By the time I got outside, the driver had already put my one large suitcase into the boot. I got in the front seat, remembering that this was Australia and a passenger was expected to sit in the front with the driver and not in the back like Royalty. And maybe not even then. This was, after all, Western Australia.

I had taken the view for a while that WA was quite different to the rest of the country in many ways. A couple of days earlier in Perth's smart new CBD I had eavesdropped on a couple of Sydney bankers who were over in Perth for a conference. They were seated at a table next to mine, drinking coffee and munching on a steak sandwich that Desperate Dan would have been proud of.

'Tell you what, mate, I just can't believe how this place has grown. None of this was here a decade ago.'

'Yeah, tell me, mate. It's like bloody California over here. I just can't believe it. I might bring the missus over next time. If there is a next time.'

'Well let's just make sure there bloody is, mate.'

And that in a nutshell sums up, as I see it, how WA sits within the whole of Australia. The rush to California, the richest state in America, was initially fuelled by gold. In a similar manner the rush to WA is fuelled by mountains of iron ore, not to mention a dollop or two of gold. Isolated by two thousand miles of desert and Bight from the Establishment in the east, WA is probably the only State that could stand alone from the Commonwealth and still get richer. The mandarins in Canberra would do well to remember that. Meanwhile, back to the taxi.

'It's a beautiful evening. I checked your flight time – Emirates to Dubai, yeah?' Lynne had booked the cab for me.

'There's plenty of time. I'll take you on the scenic route. No extra charge mate, no worries.'

We headed north first and picked up the Reid Highway, turning east and then south. To our right in the west the sun had just dipped into the Indian Ocean, leaving an artist's palette of gold, yellow and orange as far as you could see. Magically, to our left a full moon had already risen above the higher ground, illuminating the landscape. Turning my head left, right and then left again to take in two contrasting skyscapes, I felt like a spectator at a tennis match.

'It's your lucky night, mate, a perfect sunset and a full moon. Can't say I've ever seen it quite like this before myself.'

'Are you a Perthite? My last taxi driver was a Somali refo with a sat nav.' He chuckled.

'Yeah, there's a few of those, mate. Yes, I'm a Perthite. Born and bred. Was this your first visit to Australia?'

'Yes, I flew into Perth, then after a while hopped over to Queensland to visit cousins. Actually, they used to live here in WA but moved, first to Tassie, then to Queensland.'

'Oh well, we all make mistakes, mate.'

'What is that high ground called under the moon? Does it have a name?'

'Yeah, it's roughly in the area of Gooseberry Hill.'

'I grow gooseberries back home. Have you ever tried them?'

'No way. Nothing grows in the sand here, mate. What are they like?'

'Like a green marble, hard and quite tart. There's a famous pudding called Gooseberry Fool.'

'No way. Maybe they should rename it Fool on the Hill, eh?'

This guy had a sense of humour and obviously remembered the Beatles tune of the same name. I probed a bit further.

'Are you second generation Oz, mind me asking?'

'Yep. Mum and Dad came over in the first wave of 'ten pound Poms' in the early sixties. More Poms have come to WA than any other State, so they say, anyway.'

'Is that why some folk call Perth a Pommy ghetto?'

'I wouldn't say that, mate. But I think most of your mob come over here to get out of the cold. And to learn how to play cricket properly!'

We both laughed. He probably had a point there. And on the subject of cricket I suddenly saw a signpost announcing a turn-off to Lesmurdie. Instantly a memory flashed back.

'See that sign, Lesmurdie? Well, a few years back during a Test Match, I think at Lords, a good shot screamed to the boundary for four runs. As the camera zoomed in to catch the fielder retrieving the ball, a spectator threw an Aussie flag over the advertising hoarding and underneath in huge letters he'd written 'Hello Lesmurdie.'

'No way, that's where I live!'

'Really? Crikey! Anyway, get this. The commentator at that precise moment of play was Richie Benaud, and you know what a dry sense of humour he has.'

'What did he say?'

He said, 'for those of you not familiar with Western Australia, Lesmurdie is a suburb of Perth, not a bloke.'

'That sounds like Richie. Anyway, we're almost here, mate, the International Terminal, I mean.'

We got out and I paid the fare and a few bucks extra for a Swan Lager or two.

'Safe journey, mate. Come back again won't you? And maybe watch a proper cricket team next time!'

Those parting words were the same as the first ones spoken to me in Australia. 'Come back and see us again.' So I did.